This cookbook is
FROM the KITCHEN of

_____

peace meals

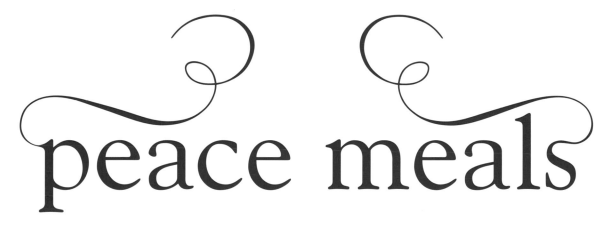

peace meals

A BOOK *of* RECIPES *for* COOKING *and* CONNECTING

A COOKBOOK *by*
The JUNIOR LEAGUE *of* HOUSTON, *Inc.*
Generously supported by
Central Market

dedication

To those who pause for timeless moments
in the rush of here and now;

to those who've had their breath taken away
by the ecstasy of a chocolate mousse or a tart, crisp apple;

to those who recall the best moments of their existence
and purposely set out to create more;

to those who do and to those who try;

to those who appreciate the changing seasons
and yet keep loving the same people, year in, year out;

to our children and our parents,
our friends and our true sweethearts;

to the people, places and pieces of our lives,
WE LOVINGLY DEDICATE THIS BOOK.

foreword

Who has not, at least once, thought that life in our grandmothers' time moved

to rhythms we can no longer quite hear? With comfortable predictability,

family houses were cleaned and aired out every spring, peaches "put up"

late each summer, winter days made bright with rites of celebration and renewal.

And just as holidays and seasonal tasks paced the years, carefully measured

portions of work and sleep and play paced the days. Woven throughout it all,

nuanced rituals of preparing and serving food marked time's orderly passing:

breakfast signaled each day's start as surely as Sunday supper meant pot roast, and

the annual stuffed turkey expressed a collectively-offered thanks. The patterns

that emerged seemed evidence of lives cut from good, whole cloth.

Not so of our lives today. Just as vibrant, but lighter on ritual and routine, the lives most of us lead are a whole lot more piecemeal than pattern. Good lives, no doubt. But it is easy to wonder, if only in passing, whether all those lovely pieces form anything resembling a perfect whole.

Which, of course, they *do*.

Because daily life is where Life happens. And inside the patchwork of countless ordinary moments are moments of singular, extraordinary beauty, luminous instants of connection that, when we experience them, revive and restore our souls. Moments like these can happen anywhere at any time, but it is not surprising that peace so often steals over us when we are gathered together around a table breaking bread.

For even if meals punctuate our days with less ritual than they did our grandmothers', an ever-present thread running through our lives is food. It is the instrument of physical regeneration, a biological necessity. We eat to live. But there is more to it than that. Food prepared with mindfulness and intent, and eaten with thought and thanksgiving, satisfies hungers that are deeper than those of the body.

Our first and most basic needs are, after all, for food and for touch—
we reach out for them the minute we're born. Later, it is at the table
that we as children begin to learn life's most important lessons:
grace and courtesy, the art of conversation, the responsibility that comes
with choice. The table is where we come to know our own appetites
and to cultivate an awareness of what truly fulfills us. As adults we share
a meal when we want to mend a fence, seal a deal, celebrate a passage,
fall in love or simply take a pleasurable break from life's clutter with
a friend. We share food to connect.

And nourishing connection is what this book is about.

The recipes in these pages, some fancy, some simple, are our best.
More than a collection of cooking how-tos, though, this is a book about
life. The recipes are only breadcrumbs along a path to the greater human
experience, of which food—so necessary, so satisfying—is just a piece.

Mary Frances Kennedy Fisher, poet laureate of dining, wrote that
a good book about food is "as much touched with the spirit as the bread and
meat and wine with which it deals." We hope you will find this such a book.

contents

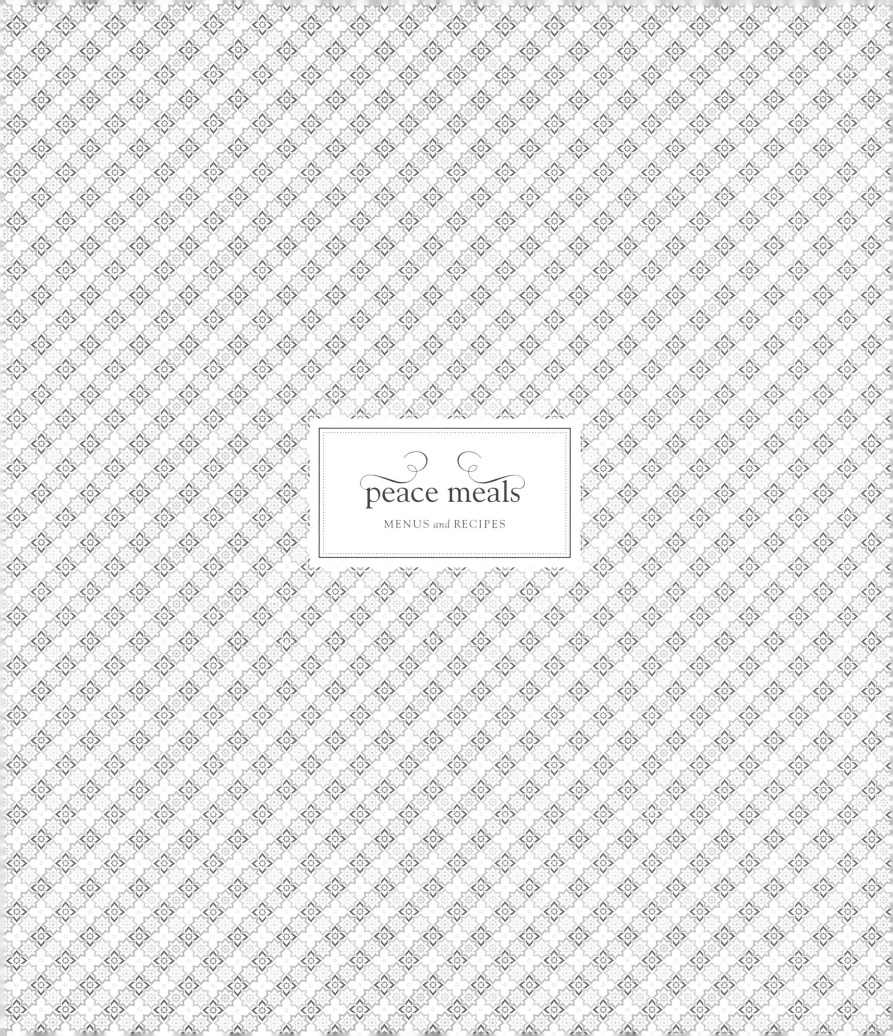

peace meals

MENUS *and* RECIPES

breakfast a

...nd brunch

menu sampler

WEEKEND HOUSEGUESTS

Arugula and Asparagus Frittata

Brown Sugar Bacon Twists

Cinnamon Pear Scones

Cherry Almond Granola

Hot Coffee and Fresh Orange Juice

Whole Fruit Basket

❧

COUNTRY BRUNCH

*Ranch Style Eggs with
Chorizo and Tomato Red Chile Sauce*

*Oatmeal Cake served with
Fruit and Fresh Whipped Cream*

Spicy Rosemary Cashews

Jalapeño Cheese Biscuits

*Watermelon Mango Salsa served
with Blue Tortilla Chips*

White Wine Sangria

El Diablo

❧

SUNRISE CELEBRATION

Herbed Eggs with Sautéed Arugula

Crème Brûlée French Toast

Blueberry Pine Nut Coffee Cake

Grits

Fresh Berries and Sliced Fruit

Mimosas

country brunch

country brunch

In the city, we tend to awaken reluctantly and rush off to breakfast still yawning. But not so in the country. Here, the sun's first bright rays find a table under the oak tree being laid for breakfast, cut glass goblets waiting to be filled with freshly squeezed orange juice. Children take turns on the rope swing as guests begin to amble outside. Shadows will grow shorter, and then longer again, before anyone thinks of saying goodbye.

White Wine Sangria, PAGE 71

country brunch

DETAILS

Invitations
Texas Pecan Tree saplings
wrapped in burlap, hand delivered,
with details and a map
tied on with ribbon.

Favors
Spicy Rosemary Cashews in
mini country-style galvanized tubs
wrapped in netting or muslin.

For Fun
A tour of the ranch's beautiful
fall foliage via tractor-drawn hayride,
with piles of quilts on hand
for a chilly morning.

Spicy Rosemary Cashews, PAGE 66

country brunch

TIPS

The day before, watch the sun's path to find the right place (not too shady, not too sunny) for the table.

Bring indoor tables, chairs and even rugs outside to create an al fresco dining room.

Weight the tablecloth corners, even if the day starts with no breeze. Things change.

Forgo paper and plastic and use the "good stuff."

Use small tables and chairs, picnic blankets and pillows to create inviting gathering spots away from the table.

Oatmeal Cake, PAGE 40

Ranch Style Eggs with Chorizo and Tomato Red Chile Sauce, PAGE 29

ITALIAN STYLE POACHED EGGS

SERVES 4

This colorful and savory egg dish is perfect for a lingering, late morning breakfast with family or friends.
Delicious with cappuccino and mini Almond Polenta Muffins (page 34).

3 small ripe tomatoes, cut into ¼-inch slices
½ teaspoon dried oregano
1½ teaspoons chopped fresh basil
2 tablespoons freshly grated Parmesan cheese,
  plus additional
2 tablespoons butter
2 English muffins, sliced and toasted
4 eggs, poached (page 114)

coarse salt and freshly ground pepper
Creamed Spinach (recipe below)
6 slices bacon, cooked and crumbled

✑ CREAMED SPINACH ∾

2 tablespoons butter
1 tablespoon grated onion
9 ounces fresh spinach
½ cup sour cream
1 cup freshly grated Parmesan cheese
1 tablespoon all-purpose flour
2 eggs, beaten
coarse salt and freshly ground pepper

Melt the butter in a medium skillet; add the onion and spinach, and sauté until wilted. Add the sour cream, cheese, flour and eggs. Season with salt and pepper, and cook until thickened.

Preheat the oven to broil. Place the tomatoes in a 9 by 9-inch baking dish; sprinkle with the oregano, basil and cheese, and dot with the butter. Broil for 2 minutes. Top each muffin half with tomato slices. Place a poached egg on top of the tomato and season with salt and pepper. Top each egg with the *Creamed Spinach* and bacon. Sprinkle with additional cheese.

RANCH STYLE EGGS *with* CHORIZO *and* TOMATO RED CHILE SAUCE

SERVES 6 to 8

Made from dried ripe poblano peppers, ancho chiles have a deep, rich peppery flavor with a slight chocolate undertone.
This classic Mexican Tomato Red Chile Sauce can also be served over grilled flank steak or chicken.

Tomato Red Chile Sauce:
2 tablespoons olive oil
1 large red onion, coarsely chopped
4 cloves garlic, coarsely chopped
1 cup dry red wine
3 cups (24 ounces) canned tomato purée
2 tablespoons ancho chile powder
1 tablespoon pasilla chile powder
2 tablespoons honey
coarse salt

Eggs:
canola oil
6 to 8 (6-inch) yellow or white corn tortillas
coarse salt and freshly ground pepper
8 ounces Mexican chorizo sausage, casings removed
4 tablespoons unsalted butter, cut into tablespoons
12 eggs, lightly beaten with 2 tablespoons water
⅔ cup sour cream
¾ cup shredded Monterey Jack cheese
chopped fresh cilantro
1 avocado, pitted, peeled and chopped

Heat the olive oil in a medium saucepan over medium-high. Sauté the onions, stirring until softened. Add the garlic and cook for 1 minute. Add the wine and cook until completely reduced. Stir in the tomato purée, chile powders and honey; season with salt. Cook over medium-high heat until the sauce has thickened, stirring occasionally, about 20 to 30 minutes. Set aside.

Pour the oil in a medium skillet to a depth of 2 inches. Heat to 360°F over medium-high. Fry the tortillas, turning once, until lightly golden brown on both sides. Drain on paper towels and season immediately with salt. Heat a large skillet over medium-high; add the chorizo and brown, using a spoon to break up the meat. Remove the chorizo with a slotted spoon to a paper towel-lined plate and let cool slightly. Drain all but 1 tablespoon of the chorizo drippings and add the butter to the pan. Once the butter is melted, turn the heat to medium-low, add the eggs and season with salt and pepper. Cook over medium-low heat for 10 to 15 minutes, stirring frequently, until the mixture resembles soft curds. Return the chorizo to the pan and stir gently to mix, making sure the chorizo is in small pieces. Place 1 teaspoon of sour cream in each of 6 to 8 large shallow bowls to secure the tortillas. Top each dollop of sour cream with a tortilla, then spread 1 tablespoon of sour cream on the top of each tortilla. Place equal portions of eggs on each tortilla and ladle the warm *Tomato Red Chile Sauce* over the eggs. Sprinkle each with the cheese, cilantro and avocado.

HERBED EGGS *with* SAUTÉED ARUGULA

SERVES 4

These dressed up scrambled eggs can be served family style. Arrange the arugula on a serving platter and top with the eggs.
Fresh chervil can be substituted for the tarragon for a slightly different flavor.

10 eggs
¼ cup milk
coarse salt and freshly ground pepper
¼ cup garlic and herb feta cheese
¼ cup mascarpone cheese
1 tablespoon minced fresh tarragon, plus additional

1½ tablespoons butter
1 tablespoon olive oil
1 garlic clove, pressed
4 to 6 cups arugula

Whisk together the eggs and milk in a large bowl; season with salt and pepper. In a separate small bowl, mix together the feta, mascarpone and tarragon. Melt the butter in a large heavy skillet over medium heat. Add the eggs and cook until almost set, stirring occasionally. Meanwhile, heat the olive oil in a separate skillet over medium. Add the garlic and arugula, and sauté until the arugula is wilted; set aside. Add the cheese mixture to the eggs and stir until the cheese is melted and the eggs are softly set. Divide the arugula among 4 plates and top with the eggs. Garnish with additional tarragon.

ELEGANT EGG STRATA

SERVES 8 *to* 12

The rich, velvety sauce is what makes this dish special. Because it can be prepared the night before,
it is practical for even the most elegant gathering—morning or evening.

30

Sauce:
3 tablespoons butter
1 clove garlic, pressed
¼ cup chopped onion
3 tablespoons all-purpose flour
1½ cups chicken broth
¾ cup dry white wine
pinch of ground nutmeg
pinch of dry mustard
coarse salt and freshly ground pepper
½ cup sour cream

Eggs:
3 cups cubed French bread
3 tablespoons butter, melted
2 cups shredded Swiss or Gruyère cheese
½ cup freshly grated Parmesan cheese
8 eggs
snipped fresh chives, for garnish

This recipe requires overnight preparation. Melt the butter in a medium saucepan and sauté the garlic and onion until soft. Add the flour and stir to combine; cook until light golden. Stir in the broth, wine, nutmeg and mustard; season with salt and pepper. Bring to a boil, reduce heat and simmer for 15 minutes, stirring occasionally. Remove from heat and stir in the sour cream. Taste and adjust the seasonings as needed. Set aside.

Butter a 9 by 13-inch baking dish. Place the bread cubes in the dish and pour the melted butter evenly over the bread; sprinkle with all the cheese. Mix the eggs and reserved sauce in a food processor. Pour the mixture over the bread and cheese. Cover with plastic wrap and refrigerate overnight. Remove from the refrigerator 1 hour before baking. Preheat the oven to 350°F. Uncover and bake for about 30 minutes or until set. Garnish with chives and serve immediately.

Herbed Eggs with Sautéed Arugula, PAGE 30

ARUGULA and ASPARAGUS FRITTATA

SERVES 2

Frittatas are open-faced Italian style omelets that can be filled with a variety of meats, cheeses and vegetables.
They are often served at breakfast but, served with a green salad, are substantial enough for a weeknight dinner.

4 eggs
2 tablespoons milk
1 teaspoon minced fresh thyme
coarse salt and freshly ground pepper
1 tablespoon butter

4 asparagus spears, ends trimmed, cut into 1-inch pieces
½ cup shredded Gruyère cheese
2 cups arugula
1 tablespoon freshly grated Parmesan cheese

Preheat the oven to broil. Beat together the eggs, milk and thyme. Season with salt and pepper; set aside. Melt the butter in a 10-inch nonstick, ovenproof skillet over medium heat. Sauté the asparagus until crisp tender, about 4 minutes. Combine the asparagus and Gruyère in a small bowl; set aside. In the same skillet, sauté the arugula until wilted, about 1 minute. Reduce heat to medium-low and pour the egg mixture over the arugula. Cook until the bottom is set and the top is still wet, about 4 minutes. Top with the asparagus mixture. Place the skillet under the broiler and cook until the frittata is golden, about 2 to 4 minutes. Sprinkle with the Parmesan and serve warm or at room temperature.

FRITTATA with FONTINA and ITALIAN SAUSAGE

SERVES 8

Mustard greens (rich in vitamins) add a peppery flavor to this frittata.
While at their best December through April, mustard greens can usually be found throughout the year.

8 ounces mild Italian sausage, casings removed
½ cup chopped onion
1½ cups chopped fresh mustard greens
¾ cup chopped tomatoes

coarse salt and freshly ground pepper
12 eggs
½ cup heavy whipping cream
1 cup shredded Fontina cheese

Preheat the oven to 450°F. Brown the sausage in a 10 or 12-inch nonstick, ovenproof skillet over medium heat until cooked through, about 5 minutes; use a spoon to break apart the meat. Add the onion and cook until softened, about 2 more minutes. Stir in the greens and tomatoes, and season with salt and pepper. Cook until the greens are wilted, about 1 to 2 minutes. Remove the sausage mixture from the skillet and set aside. Wipe out the skillet and coat generously with cooking spray. Mix the eggs, cream and 1 teaspoon of salt in a blender until frothy. Return the skillet to medium heat. Pour in the egg mixture and cook just until curds form, stirring constantly. Stir in the sausage mixture and add the cheese. Transfer the skillet to the oven and bake for 12 to 18 minutes or until set in the center. Loosen the edges of the frittata and slide onto a plate. Slice into wedges and serve warm or at room temperature.

BROWN SUGAR BACON TWISTS

MAKES 16 SLICES

This peppery bacon adds a delightful twist to any breakfast (and try it on a BLT or a burger).
As a sweeter alternative, replace the brown sugar and pepper with ⅓ cup sugar and 1 tablespoon cinnamon.
Use thinly sliced bacon to make sure the twists hold.

1 pound bacon (16 slices)
⅓ cup firmly packed light brown sugar
2 teaspoons freshly ground pepper

Preheat the oven to 350°F. Line a rimmed baking sheet with aluminum foil; place a wire rack on top of the sheet. Arrange the bacon in a single layer on the rack. Sprinkle the bacon evenly with the sugar and pepper. Tightly twist each slice to form a spiral. Bake until the bacon is crisp and browned, about 30 to 35 minutes.

SAVORY BREAD PUDDING *with* SAUSAGE *and* GREENS

SERVES 6 *to* 8

Use almost any type of crusty bread (fresh or a few days old) and almost any green (chard, kale, escarole)
to make this hearty and fast bread pudding. It can be assembled the day before, covered and refrigerated until time to bake.
Bring the dish to room temperature before baking, or increase the baking time by 10 to 15 minutes if baked cold.

½ tablespoon butter
2 tablespoons olive oil
1 large onion, cut in half and thinly sliced
   (about 1½ cups)
2 cloves garlic, minced or pressed (about 2 teaspoons)
1 pound fresh mild Italian sausage,
   casings removed and crumbled
2 cups arugula

2 cups (1 pint) milk
4 eggs
1 cup shredded Gruyère cheese
1 pound French or country bread, cubed into
   2-inch pieces
1 teaspoon coarse salt
½ teaspoon freshly ground pepper
⅛ teaspoon freshly grated nutmeg

Preheat the oven to 375°F. Coat a 9 by 13-inch baking dish with the butter. Heat the olive oil in a large skillet over medium-high. Add the onions and sauté until soft and slightly golden, about 5 minutes. Add the garlic and stir. Immediately add the crumbled sausage to the pan and sauté until cooked through and no longer pink, about 5 to 10 minutes; use a spoon to break up the meat if necessary. Add the arugula to the sausage mixture, reduce heat to low and stir until wilted. Remove the pan from heat. In a large bowl, whisk together the milk and eggs. Stir in the cheese, cubed bread and seasonings. Add the sausage mixture to the bowl and stir to combine. Pour the mixture into the prepared baking dish and bake uncovered for about 45 minutes, or until the top is golden and a knife inserted in the middle comes out almost clean. If the top is brown after 30 minutes, cover with foil and continue to bake until the center is cooked.

CRÈME BRÛLÉE FRENCH TOAST

SERVES 8

Challah is a soft and rich Jewish yeast bread made with eggs and butter, often made as a braided loaf.
In this recipe, brioche or croissants can be substituted. This dish is even more colorful and delicious served with seasonal berries.

¾ cup (1½ sticks) butter
1½ cups firmly packed brown sugar
3 tablespoons corn syrup
1 loaf challah bread, sliced 1-inch thick
   with each piece sliced in half diagonally
6 eggs
2 cups (1 pint) half-and-half
2 cups (1 pint) milk
1 teaspoon pure vanilla extract

⅓ cup sugar
½ teaspoon salt
1 teaspoon Grand Marnier® (optional)
powdered sugar, for dusting

This recipe requires advance preparation. Lightly butter a 9 by 13-inch baking dish and set aside. Melt the butter and brown sugar with the corn syrup in a small saucepan over medium heat; stir until smooth and bubbly. Pour the mixture into the prepared dish. Arrange the bread slices on top in two overlapping rows, slightly stacking the bread. In a large bowl, whisk together the eggs, half-and-half, milk, vanilla, sugar, salt and liqueur until well combined; pour evenly over the bread. Cover with foil and chill for at least 8 hours or overnight. Preheat the oven to 350°F. Bake until set in the center, approximately 45 minutes, then uncover and bake an additional 15 minutes or until golden brown. Dust with powdered sugar and serve with the sauce from the dish.

RASPBERRY WHITE CHOCOLATE MUFFINS

MAKES 12 MUFFINS

These easy to make muffins are as tasty and beautiful as cupcakes.
Overmixing the batter makes muffins tough, so use only 10 to 15 strokes to incorporate the dry ingredients.

⅓ cup butter, softened
½ cup sugar, plus additional
2 eggs
1 cup plain yogurt
1 cup white chocolate chips

2 cups all-purpose flour
2 teaspoons baking powder
1 teaspoon salt
½ pint fresh raspberries

Preheat the oven to 350°F. Coat muffin pans with nonstick cooking spray. Cream together the butter and sugar in a large bowl. Add the eggs one at a time, mixing well after each addition. Add the yogurt, then the white chocolate chips. Stir in the flour, baking powder and salt (the batter will be stiff). Gently fold in the raspberries. Spoon the mixture into the prepared muffin cups; sprinkle with sugar. Bake for 22 to 24 minutes or until golden brown. Cool the muffins in the pan for 5 minutes, then remove and cool completely on a wire rack.

> ❧ GIFTS *from the* KITCHEN ❧
>
> - *Muffins, scones, breads and granolas make thoughtful gifts for a hostess who will be happy to wake up to a homemade breakfast, ready and waiting in a pretty package.*
>
> - *When you want to thank someone for kind deeds or hard work, a tin of cookies or spiced nuts is an especially personal expression of appreciation.*
>
> - *Infused oils, salts and sugars make unique and memorable parting gifts for houseguests and party guests.*

ALMOND POLENTA MUFFINS

MAKES 12 MUFFINS

An easy choice for breakfast or brunch, these sweet corn muffins are equally at home with a salad or bowl of soup.
Serve them plain, with jam or whipped cream, or try drizzling them with honey.

½ cup cake flour
½ cup cornmeal
¾ teaspoon baking powder
¼ teaspoon salt
¾ cup (6 ounces) almond paste

½ cup sugar
⅝ cup (1¼ sticks) unsalted butter, softened
1 teaspoon pure vanilla extract
2 eggs, plus 2 egg yolks

Preheat the oven to 350°F. Lightly butter muffin pans. Stir together the flour, cornmeal, baking powder and salt; set aside. Place the almond paste and sugar in the bowl of a stand mixer fitted with a paddle attachment. Beat at medium speed until the mixture is crumbly, about 2 minutes. Scrape the bowl and paddle; add the butter and beat on medium speed until the mixture is smooth, about 2 minutes. Scrape the bowl again and add the vanilla. Beat until well blended. Add the whole eggs and egg yolks one at a time and beat until the mixture is very smooth and fluffy, about 2 minutes. Stir in the flour mixture. Pour the batter evenly into the prepared muffin cups. Bake for 20 to 25 minutes or until the muffins spring back when lightly pressed in the center. Cool for 10 minutes on a wire rack before removing from the pan.

APPLE PECAN MUFFINS
MAKES 18 MUFFINS
These chunky muffins have the tried-and-true flavor of cinnamon, nutmeg and apples.

½ cup (1 stick) unsalted butter, softened
2 cups sugar, plus additional
2 eggs
1 teaspoon pure vanilla extract
2½ cups all-purpose flour
1 teaspoon baking powder
¾ teaspoon baking soda

1 teaspoon salt
1 teaspoon cinnamon
½ teaspoon nutmeg
3 cups peeled and diced Granny Smith or
   Jonagold apples
1 cup chopped pecans

Preheat the oven to 350°F. Butter and flour muffin pans. Cream the butter and sugar in a large bowl with an electric mixer. Add the eggs and vanilla and beat until fluffy. In a separate bowl, combine the flour, baking powder, baking soda, salt, cinnamon and nutmeg. Using a spatula, gradually add the dry ingredients to the creamed mixture; do not over mix (the batter will be thick). Fold in the apples and pecans. Spoon the batter into the prepared muffin cups and sprinkle with additional sugar. Bake for 25 minutes. Cool the muffins in the pan for 5 minutes, then remove and let cool completely on a wire rack.

SUGAR *and* SPICE *and* EVERYTHING NICE LOAF BREAD
MAKES 1 LOAF
This is an easy recipe with a long list of ingredients that add flavor, not time.
Consider toasting a slice of this delicious loaf bread and topping with whipped cream cheese.

1½ cups all-purpose flour
1 teaspoon baking powder
1 teaspoon baking soda
½ teaspoon salt
½ teaspoon cinnamon
¼ teaspoon nutmeg
¼ teaspoon ground ginger
⅛ teaspoon ground allspice
½ cup sugar
¼ cup molasses

1 egg
¼ cup buttermilk
¼ cup freshly squeezed orange juice
¼ cup vegetable oil
1 tablespoon finely grated orange zest
½ teaspoon pure vanilla extract
15 ounces canned crushed pineapple, drained
¾ cup peeled and finely grated carrots
½ cup golden raisins
½ cup chopped walnuts, toasted

Preheat the oven to 350°F. Spray a 9 by 5-inch loaf pan with cooking spray. Sift together the flour, baking powder, baking soda, salt, spices and sugar into a large bowl. In a medium bowl, whisk together the molasses, egg, buttermilk, orange juice, oil, zest and vanilla; stir in the pineapple. Pour the liquid mixture into the flour mixture and stir until just combined. Fold in the carrots, raisins and walnuts. Pour the batter into the prepared pan; bake for 55 minutes to 1 hour 10 minutes or until a toothpick inserted in the center comes out clean. Cool the bread in the pan for 5 minutes, then remove from the pan and let cool completely on a wire rack. Slice with a serrated knife.

> ### ✑ ALLSPICE ✒
> *Allspice is aptly named, since it tastes like a combination of pepper, clove, cinnamon and nutmeg. The allspice tree is an evergreen with thin, pale yellow bark that peels away annually. Its white flowers appear in small clusters bearing round berries which have a sweet pungent taste and an intense scent. This spice is sold in whole or ground form by most grocery stores.*

CINNAMON PEAR SCONES

MAKES 15 LARGE *or* 30 SMALL SCONES

Scones, a traditional British quick bread, are incredibly versatile. Sweet or savory, large or small,
scones are delicious for breakfast or an indulgent snack. They also make a unique accompaniment to soups and salads.

1 cup (2 sticks) plus 3 tablespoons unsalted butter,
   softened, divided
1 cup peeled and diced fresh pears
1 cup plus 1 tablespoon sugar, divided, plus additional
2 tablespoons plus ½ teaspoon cinnamon, divided

8 cups all-purpose flour
3 tablespoons baking powder
1 tablespoon salt
2½ to 3 cups heavy whipping cream

Preheat the oven to 400°F. Line baking sheets with parchment paper. Melt 1 tablespoon of the butter in a small skillet over medium heat. Stir in the pears, 1 tablespoon of the sugar and ½ teaspoon of the cinnamon and sauté until the pears are softened; set aside. Mix together the flour, the remaining cup of sugar, the baking powder, the remaining 2 tablespoons of cinnamon and the salt in a large bowl. Using a fork, mix in 1 cup of the butter. Add the cream and mix by hand (up to 3 total cups of cream can be added until the dough is sticky). Add the cooled pears to the dough and gently fold in by hand. Form the dough into 4-inch discs and place on the prepared baking sheets. Bake the scones for about 30 minutes or until light golden brown. For smaller scones, form the dough into 30 2-inch discs and reduce baking time to approximately 18 to 20 minutes. Melt the remaining 2 tablespoons of butter and brush the top of each scone; generously sprinkle the scones with additional sugar.

> ⌒ SCONE IDEAS ⌒
>
> *The basic scone recipe (above) can be used to create many*
> *different scones; just replace the pears and cinnamon with other*
> *delicious combinations such as:*
>
> * *Lemon zest and blueberry*
> * *Mini chocolate chips and pecans or orange zest*
> * *Apple, cheddar and smoked bacon*
> * *Parmesan cheese and rosemary*
> * *Sun-dried tomatoes, pine nuts and basil*

JALAPEÑO CHEESE BISCUITS

INSPIRED *by the* CORONADO CLUB'S JALAPEÑO BISCUITS

MAKES 20 2-INCH BISCUITS

The secret to flaky biscuits is to use very cold butter (20 minutes in the freezer will do it).
Try these biscuits with scrambled eggs for a spicy start to your day.

2 cups all-purpose flour
2 tablespoons sugar
¼ teaspoon salt
¼ teaspoon white pepper
1 tablespoon baking powder
dash of cayenne pepper

½ cup (1 stick) cold unsalted butter
1 tablespoon cored, seeded and finely chopped jalapeño
   (or 2 tablespoons snipped fresh chives)
¾ cup shredded cheddar cheese
1¼ cups heavy whipping cream

Preheat the oven to 375°F. Line a baking sheet with parchment paper. Sift the dry ingredients into a mixing bowl. Cut the butter into ½-inch pieces. Using your fingertips, rub the butter and flour mixture together until it resembles a coarse meal; add the jalapeños and cheese. Add the cream and mix with your hands. When barely combined, turn out onto a lightly floured board and knead just enough to bring the dough together. Roll out to a 1-inch thickness. Cut with a floured 1½ to 2-inch cutter. Arrange in a single layer on the prepared baking sheet. Bake in the center of the oven for 10 to 12 minutes or until puffed and golden. Serve warm.

Cinnamon Pear Scones, PAGE 36

Gingerbread Pancakes, PAGE 39

CHERRY ALMOND GRANOLA

MAKES 8 CUPS

To make this breakfast favorite an afternoon treat, add 1 cup of mini semi-sweet chocolate chips
once the granola has cooled. The chocolate is a nice complement to the cherries.

¼ cup vegetable oil
¼ cup honey
¼ cup brown sugar
1 teaspoon pure vanilla extract
3 cups old-fashioned rolled oats

1¼ cups sliced almonds
1 cup dried cherries
1 cup sweetened flaked coconut
¼ cup flax seeds

Preheat the oven to 300°F. Line a rimmed baking sheet with parchment paper. Stir together the oil, honey, brown sugar and vanilla in a small saucepan over low heat until blended and the sugar has dissolved; keep warm. In a large bowl, mix together the oats, almonds, cherries, coconut and flax seeds. Add the warm oil-honey mixture and stir until the granola is well coated. Spread the granola on the prepared baking sheet and bake for 30 to 32 minutes or until golden brown, stirring halfway through. Cool completely, then loosen from the baking sheet and crumble. Store in an airtight container.

PEANUT BUTTER GRANOLA

MAKES 5 CUPS

This recipe is fun to make with your young chefs-in-training. Serve with fresh apples and blueberries, and add milk or yogurt.

2 cups old-fashioned rolled oats
1 cup wheat germ or wheat bran
1 cup oat bran
½ cup sunflower seed kernels
½ cup hulled pumpkin seeds (pepitas)
½ cup unsweetened shredded or flaked coconut

½ cup slivered almonds
2 teaspoons cinnamon
1 cup creamy peanut butter
½ cup honey
1 cup chopped dried fruit, such as apricots,
   apples or raisins (optional)

43

Preheat the oven to 300°F. Line two rimmed baking sheets with parchment paper. Combine the oats, wheat germ, oat bran, seeds, coconut, almonds and cinnamon in a large bowl. Add the peanut butter and honey, and combine by hand until the mixture is well coated. Spread the mixture evenly over the baking sheets. Bake, stirring every 5 minutes, until light golden brown, about 20 minutes. Allow the granola to cool to room temperature. Stir in the dried fruit if desired. Store in an airtight container.

appetizers

nd cocktails

menu sampler

SIMPLY WINE *and* CHEESE

A selection of
artisan cheeses, crusty breads
and crackers, fruits, chocolate
and tasting wines

COCKTAIL PARTY

Pomegranate Martini

Gulf Coast Ceviche

White Bean Dip with
Lemon Sage Olive Oil

Endive with Caramelized
Apples and Pears

Maple Salmon Bites

Indian-Spiced Pork and
Red Grape Brochettes

Pommes Frites with
Truffle Oil and Parmesan

A SPIRITED AFFAIR

Champagne

Savory Pear and Chèvre Pastries
with Lemon and Thyme

Crostini Tapenade

Grilled Lamb with
Savory Mint Relish

Buckwheat Pancakes with Caviar

Bite-Size Bourbon Cakes

Hazelnut Dream Cookies

cocktail party

Champagne Pomegranate Punch, PAGE 70

cocktail party

Cocktail parties are sophisticated, spirited fun. Whether a celebratory occasion, a gathering of friends at the end of a day, or the warm-up to an evening ahead, a cocktail party is an elegantly uncomplicated affair. Food and drink are to be savored, to surprise and delight, to please … and to whet appetites for lighthearted mingling.

Gulf Coast Ceviche, PAGE 53

Pommes Frites with Truffle Oil and Parmesan, PAGE 215

Just Add Friends

cocktail party

DETAILS

Invitations
Simple, chic cards tucked into
martini shakers invite guests to mix
it up with friends old and new.

Favors
Cinnamon Pear Scones packed
in shiny silver tins offer your guests
an easy breakfast the morning
after a late night.

Décor
Eclectic collections of corkscrews,
vintage soda bottles, sparkling silver
and crystal glassware—all beautifully
functional—create an alluring
ambience by candlelight.

cocktail party

TIPS

Make ahead or room temperature appetizers keep you out of the kitchen and with your guests.

Plan 3 to 6 different appetizers (10 to 12 bite-size nibbles per person), and 3 to 4 drinks per person.

Stagger appetizers for new tastes throughout the evening; place some out for self-service and pass others on trays.

Hired bartenders help, as do signature drink stations where guests serve themselves.

Guests typically use 3 to 4 glasses each; renting glassware simplifies setup and cleanup.

Don't forget ice, and plenty of it.

White Bean Dip with Lemon Sage Olive Oil PAGE 53

Mango and Black-Eyed Pea Salsa, PAGE 56

Winter Guacamole, PAGE 59

❧ SEEDING POMEGRANATES ❧

- Before starting, put on an apron and cover the work surface since the juice leaves indelible red stains.

- Starting at the crown, cut halfway through the pomegranate then pry it into two halves. (Use your fingers more than the knife to keep the seeds intact.)

- Next, cut each half again and pry the pieces apart, creating a total of four wedges.

- Working over a large bowl of water, separate the seeds from the membrane, letting loose seeds fall into the bowl. (Doing this in the sink with your hands underwater keeps those red stains off your countertop and, maybe, your hands.)

- Seeds sink and membranes float, so when you have finished separating them, it is easy to skim the membranes off the top and strain out all the seeds.

WINTER GUACAMOLE

SERVES 6

Enjoy this festive take on guacamole during the holiday season when fresh pomegranates are readily available.

⅓ cup minced white onion
2 to 4 serrano chiles (including seeds), minced
1 teaspoon coarse salt
3 to 4 large ripe avocados, pitted, peeled and coarsely
  chopped (about 2 pounds)
3 tablespoons fresh lime juice

¾ cup peeled and diced pear
¾ cup red seedless grapes, halved
¾ cup pomegranate seeds, divided
  (about 1 to 2 pomegranates)
tortilla chips

Combine the onions, chiles and salt in a large bowl, forming a rough paste. Fold in the avocados and lime juice. Add the pears, grapes and ½ cup of the pomegranate seeds. Place in a serving dish and top with the remaining pomegranate seeds. Serve the guacamole with tortilla chips.

AVOCADO TOMATILLO SALSA

MAKES ABOUT 4 CUPS

Tomatillos are friendlier than they look—the rough husk is just a wrapper for the sweetish green fruit.
This salsa is served as a dip, but it is also delicious atop grilled fish and Mexican dishes.

5 medium tomatillos, husked and rinsed
4 medium avocados, pitted, peeled and
  coarsely chopped (about 4 cups)
1 to 2 jalapeños, seeded and minced
2 tablespoons fresh lime juice

½ teaspoon minced garlic
½ cup chopped fresh cilantro
¾ teaspoon coarse salt
blue corn tortilla chips

59

Preheat the oven to 375°F. Place the tomatillos on a foil-lined baking sheet and roast in the oven for 25 minutes, turning once halfway through. Remove from the oven and let cool slightly. Coarsely chop the roasted tomatillos and combine with the avocados, jalapeños, lime juice, garlic, cilantro and salt. Serve warm or chilled with tortilla chips.

TOMATO PESTO TART

SERVES 6 *to* 8

This simple, satisfying tart is pleasing served solo or as part of a weekend brunch buffet.

1 refrigerated pie crust
2 cups shredded mozzarella cheese, divided
5 plum tomatoes, sliced
½ cup mayonnaise

¼ cup freshly grated Parmesan cheese
2 tablespoons prepared basil pesto
½ teaspoon freshly ground pepper
3 tablespoons chopped fresh basil

Preheat the oven to 425°F. Place the pie crust on a lightly oiled baking sheet. Brush the outer inch of the crust with water. Bake for 8 to 10 minutes. Remove from the oven and sprinkle with 1 cup of the mozzarella cheese, leaving about a ¾-inch border around the crust. Reduce the oven temperature to 375°F. Let the crust cool for 15 minutes. Arrange the tomato slices over the cheese. Combine the remaining 1 cup of mozzarella, the mayonnaise, Parmesan, pesto and pepper in a small bowl. Spread the mixture over the tomato slices. Bake the tart for 20 to 25 minutes. Remove from the oven and sprinkle with the basil. Slice into small wedges or strips and serve warm.

ENDIVE *with* CARAMELIZED APPLES *and* PEARS

MAKES 24 PIECES

The endive in this recipe is an elegant carrier for cheese, nuts and delicately glazed fruit.
For a different presentation, cut the apples and pears into thin slices instead of chopping them.

½ tablespoon butter
2 Granny Smith apples, cored and diced
1 Bosc pear, cored and diced
1 tablespoon sugar
3 ounces Stilton blue cheese, crumbled

2 tablespoons chopped walnuts, toasted
⅛ teaspoon coarse salt
24 Belgian endive leaves (about 3 heads)
1 teaspoon chopped fresh parsley, for garnish

Heat the butter in a large skillet over medium. Add the apples, pears and sugar, and sauté for 2 minutes or until lightly glazed. Remove from heat and let cool. In a small bowl, combine the cheese, walnuts and salt. Spoon about 1 tablespoon of the mixture into each endive leaf. Top with the caramelized fruit. Arrange on a serving platter and sprinkle with parsley to garnish.

HERBED PARMESAN GOUGÈRES

MAKES 3 DOZEN GOUGÈRES

Gougères are a classic French pastry invented in 1540. These savory, bite-size puffs are great for wine tastings
and make wonderful companions for soups and salads. Make the batter a day ahead and refrigerate it; drop the chilled batter onto
a parchment-lined baking sheet and let it come to room temperature before baking.

1 cup milk
½ cup (1 stick) butter
1 teaspoon coarse salt
1 cup all-purpose flour

5 eggs, divided
2 cups freshly grated Parmigiano-Reggiano cheese, divided
1 tablespoon snipped fresh chives

Position the rack in the center of the oven. Preheat the oven to 400°F. Line a large baking sheet with parchment paper. Combine the milk, butter and salt in a medium saucepan and bring to a boil over medium heat. Remove from heat and add the flour, whisking vigorously until the flour is incorporated; let cool for 2 to 3 minutes. Stir in 4 of the eggs, one at a time. Stir in 1½ cups of the cheese and the chives. Drop the batter by tablespoonfuls onto the prepared baking sheet, spacing the gougères about 2 inches apart. Beat the remaining egg in a small bowl and brush generously on the tops of the gougères; sprinkle with the remaining ½ cup of cheese. Bake for 10 minutes or until slightly puffed. Reduce heat to 350°F. Bake for an additional 14 to 15 minutes or until the gougères are puffed and golden brown. Serve warm or at room temperature.

MADRAS SHRIMP

SERVES 6

These exotic, flavor-packed bites are enticing as hors d'oeuvres or served over rice as an entrée.

¼ cup prepared mango chutney such as
  Major Grey's Chutney®
½ teaspoon Madras curry powder
1 tablespoon fresh lemon juice
1 tablespoon white wine
1 teaspoon peeled and minced fresh ginger
1 clove garlic, minced
2 green onions, chopped

12 jumbo gulf shrimp, peeled, deveined and butterflied
6 strips thinly sliced bacon, cut in half
1 tablespoon olive oil
1 tablespoon chopped unsalted peanuts
1 tablespoon sweetened flaked coconut
small wooden skewers

Combine the chutney, curry, lemon juice, wine, ginger, garlic and onions in a medium bowl. Add the shrimp, tossing to coat; let stand for 10 minutes. Remove the shrimp and reserve the sauce. Wrap the middle of each shrimp with a strip of bacon, stretching the bacon to make it overlap; secure with a wooden skewer. Heat the olive oil in a nonstick skillet over medium-high. Add the shrimp and sear for 2 minutes on each side or until the bacon is browned. Add the reserved sauce and reduce to a glaze, turning the shrimp once, about 1 to 2 minutes. Top with the peanuts and coconut, and serve immediately.

SOUTHWESTERN SHRIMP FRITTERS *with* CHILI GINGER SAUCE

MAKES 14 FRITTERS

These pleasantly piquant fritters elevate fried shrimp to something special.

Chili Ginger Sauce:
1 cup mayonnaise
1 teaspoon chili powder
1 tablespoon peeled and minced fresh ginger
1 tablespoon rice wine vinegar
1½ tablespoons fresh lime juice
1 tablespoon ketchup

Fritters:
1 cup tempura batter mix
¾ cup whole corn kernels, fresh or frozen and thawed

1 pound shrimp, peeled, deveined and cut into small pieces
¼ teaspoon ancho chile powder
¼ teaspoon cayenne pepper
1 clove garlic, minced
1 teaspoon minced onion
⅓ cup chopped fresh cilantro
1 teaspoon coarse salt
½ to 1 cup vegetable oil

Whisk together the sauce ingredients in a small bowl and set aside. Mix the tempura batter according to the package directions and set aside. Place a sauté pan over medium-high heat; add the corn and toast lightly. Add the shrimp and cook until opaque, about 2 to 3 minutes. Add the chili powder and cayenne; reduce heat to low. Add the garlic and cook until fragrant. Add the onion, cilantro and salt; remove from heat. Add 1 cup of the prepared tempura batter (there may be some batter left over) to the shrimp mixture and stir to coat. Do not overmix. Add the oil to a large skillet to a depth of 1½ inches and heat over medium-high. Ladle ¼ cup of batter into the pan and fry until golden on both sides (use ⅛ cup for smaller fritters). Remove to a paper towel-lined plate. Repeat with the remaining batter. Serve the fritters warm with the *Chili Ginger Sauce* on the side.

BUCKWHEAT PANCAKES *with* CAVIAR

MAKES 18 *to* 20 PANCAKES

These buckwheat pancakes are just as impressive topped with smoked salmon in place of caviar.
Sour cream is a good substitute if crème fraîche is not readily available.

Pancakes:
½ cup all-purpose flour
¼ cup buckwheat flour
1 teaspoon sugar
¼ teaspoon baking soda
¼ teaspoon coarse salt
2 eggs, separated
½ cup milk
3 tablespoons unsalted butter, melted, plus additional

Topping:
½ cup crème fraîche
2 ounces good quality caviar
1 tablespoon snipped fresh chives

Mix together the dry ingredients in a large bowl. In a separate bowl, whisk together the egg yolks and milk, and combine with the dry ingredients. Beat the egg whites in a large bowl with an electric mixer until soft peaks form; fold into the flour mixture. Fold in 3 tablespoons of the butter until the batter is smooth. Brush a 10 or 12-inch nonstick skillet lightly with butter and heat over medium until hot but not smoking. Working in batches, spoon 1 tablespoon of batter per pancake into the skillet and cook until the surface of the pancake bubbles, about 1 to 2 minutes; flip the pancake and cook 1 more minute. Transfer to a plate and cover to keep warm. Brush the skillet with butter between batches. To serve, top each pancake with a small spoonful of the crème fraîche, a small dollop of caviar and a sprinkle of chives.

INDIAN-SPICED PORK and RED GRAPE BROCHETTES
MAKES 10 to 12 SKEWERS
Make this appetizer a main course by skipping the grapes and keeping the tenderloin whole.
Marinate as directed here, and increase grilling time to 20 to 25 minutes. Great with basmati rice and Sautéed Broccoli Rabe (page 208).

Marinade:
1¾ teaspoons curry powder
¼ teaspoon ground cumin
¼ teaspoon paprika
¼ teaspoon ground coriander
⅛ teaspoon cinnamon
2 tablespoons olive oil
3 tablespoons freshly squeezed orange juice
1 clove garlic, finely chopped

Skewers:
1 pound pork tenderloin, trimmed and cut into ½-inch cubes
1 bunch seedless red grapes
coarse salt and freshly ground pepper
4-inch wooden skewers, soaked in water

Mix the marinade ingredients together in a large bowl. Add the pork pieces to the marinade and mix to coat. Cover and chill a minimum of 1 hour or up to overnight. On each skewer, place two pieces of pork and two grapes, alternating the ingredients. Cook over a hot grill or in a grill pan over medium-high heat until the pork is cooked through, about 8 to 10 minutes. Season with salt and pepper.

SAVORY PEAR and CHÈVRE PASTRIES with LEMON and THYME
MAKES 16 PASTRIES
These mouthwatering pastries deserve to be passed on your best silver tray.

62

1 tablespoon unsalted butter
2 tablespoons finely chopped pecans
2 ripe pears, peeled, cored and chopped
½ teaspoon sugar
1 tablespoon Cointreau® or other orange liqueur
1 teaspoon fresh thyme leaves

1 teaspoon freshly grated lemon zest
coarse salt and freshly ground pepper
17 ounces frozen puff pastry dough, thawed
2 ounces chèvre, softened
1 egg, beaten

Preheat the oven to 400°F. Line a baking sheet with parchment paper. Melt the butter in a medium sauté pan over medium-low heat. Add the pecans and cook for about 2 minutes. Add the pears and sugar, and sauté until soft, about 8 minutes. Stir in the Cointreau, thyme and lemon zest, and season with salt and pepper. Continue to cook until most of the liquid evaporates, about 8 minutes. Remove from heat and set aside. On a lightly floured surface, roll out the puff pastry dough. Using a 3-inch cookie cutter, cut out 16 circles. Spread a thin layer of chèvre on each circle of dough, then add about 1 tablespoon of the pear mixture to half of each. Brush the edges of the pastry dough circles with the egg. Fold the circles in half, pressing the edges with a fork to seal in the filling, making a half moon shape. Place on the prepared baking sheet and brush the top of each pastry generously with the egg. Bake for 12 minutes or until puffy and golden brown. Serve warm or at room temperature.

DATES STUFFED with MANCHEGO CHEESE
MAKES 30 PIECES
Maybe not the prettiest appetizer at your party, but certainly one of the tastiest.
Manchego cheese is used here, but goat cheese is a creamier and equally delicious substitute.

4 ounces Manchego cheese
30 pitted fresh Medjool dates

10 strips thinly sliced bacon, cut into thirds
wooden picks

Preheat the oven to 450°F. Coarsely chop the cheese and stuff into the cavity of each date. Wrap each stuffed date with a bacon strip and secure with a wooden pick. Place on a baking sheet and bake for 10 to 15 minutes or until the bacon is crisp, turning once during cooking to ensure even browning. Carefully remove the pick and serve hot or at room temperature.

Indian-Spiced Pork and Red Grape Brochettes, PAGE 62

Pancetta Medallions with Goat Cheese and Pear, PAGE 65

PANCETTA MEDALLIONS *with* GOAT CHEESE *and* PEAR

MAKES 20 PIECES

For pancetta that is the right thickness, specify a "#2 slice" at your deli counter.
The diameter of the pieces may look too big at first, but they will shrink to the right size for an appetizer as they cook.
To make the goat cheese easy to slice, freeze it for a few minutes first.

20 thin round slices pancetta (cured Italian bacon)
4 ounce goat cheese log
2 to 3 fresh pears, cored and sliced into thin wedges

Preheat the oven to 375°F. Place the pancetta slices on a rimmed baking sheet lined with parchment paper. Bake until crisp, about 12 minutes; remove to a paper towel-lined plate. Transfer to a serving platter and top each piece of pancetta with a slice of goat cheese and a slice of pear.

MAPLE SALMON BITES

MAKES ABOUT 35 PIECES

In keeping with the best of Asian culinary tradition, this appetizer is an inspired combination of sweet and spicy.
Allow enough time for the salmon to fully marinate before cooking.

1 cup pure maple syrup
⅓ cup soy sauce
1½ teaspoons peeled and minced fresh ginger
1 pound skinless salmon, bones removed and
   cut into bite-size cubes
3 tablespoons freshly ground pepper

3 tablespoons black sesame seeds
¼ cup crème fraîche
sesame rice crackers
snipped fresh chives

This recipe requires advance preparation. Combine the maple syrup, soy sauce and ginger in a resealable plastic bag. Add the salmon and toss to coat with the marinade; refrigerate for 2 hours. Preheat the oven to 450°F. Lightly oil a foil-lined baking sheet. Mix the pepper and sesame seeds in a small bowl. Press the top of each salmon piece into the pepper and sesame seed mixture, and place on the prepared pan. Bake for about 5 minutes. Spread a small amount of crème fraîche onto each of the crackers. Top each with a piece of salmon and chives. Serve immediately.

GRILLED GRUYÈRE *and* SALMON SANDWICHES

COURTESY *of the* CORONADO CLUB

MAKES 12 FINGER SANDWICHES

The grilled cheese sandwich goes uptown in this flavorful version.

8 Gruyère cheese slices
8 smoked salmon slices

8 thin slices white sourdough bread
6 tablespoons unsalted butter, softened

Preheat a griddle or large pan to medium-low. Assemble 4 sandwiches by layering the cheese and smoked salmon between the bread slices. Brush the outside of the sandwiches with the soft butter and grill them for about 2 minutes per side or until the cheese is melted. (Place a slightly heavy pan on the top of each sandwich to help flatten it while cooking.) Place the sandwiches on a cutting board, trim the crusts and cut each into 3 finger-size sandwiches.

CLASSIC BRUSCHETTA *al* POMODORO

MAKES ABOUT 24 PIECES

Bruschetta is the quintessential Italian appetizer. It needs few ingredients and is very easy to make.

1 loaf of rustic Italian bread such as ciabatta,
   cut into ½ to ¾-inch thick slices
2 to 3 cloves garlic, slightly crushed
extra virgin olive oil

Al Pomodoro:
2 medium tomatoes, chopped
¼ cup fresh basil chiffonade
¼ cup extra virgin olive oil
1 teaspoon Balsamic vinegar
coarse salt and freshly ground pepper

Preheat the oven to broil. Arrange the bread slices in a single layer on a baking sheet. Toast under the broiler until golden and crisp. Turn the slices over and toast until the second side is golden and crisp. Rub the toasted bread immediately with garlic and drizzle with olive oil. Combine the tomatoes, basil, olive oil and vinegar in a bowl. Top the bruschetta with the mixture. Season with salt and pepper.

CROSTINI TAPENADE

MAKES ABOUT 40 PIECES

Crostini (Italian for little toasts) are the foundation for countless delightful antipasti.
Here they serve as a vehicle for the earthy, olive-based tapenade.

1 thin loaf Italian bread or French baguette,
   cut into ¼ to ½-inch slices

Tapenade:
3 cloves garlic, minced
1 cup pitted Kalamata olives
1 cup pine nuts, toasted
1½ cups fresh parsley

1 teaspoon herbes de Provence
freshly ground pepper
¼ cup olive oil
½ cup shredded Parmigiano-Reggiano cheese
truffle oil
1 bunch fresh basil chiffonade

Preheat the oven to 350°F. Arrange the bread slices in a single layer on a baking sheet. Bake until lightly golden and crisp. Turn the slices over and bake until the second side is lightly golden and crisp. Remove the crostini from the oven and set aside. Place the garlic, olives, pine nuts, parsley and herbes de Provence in a food processor; season with pepper. Process until smooth, adding the olive oil slowly while the blade is running. Top each crostini with the desired amount of tapenade and Parmigiano-Reggiano; broil just until the cheese is melted. Drizzle with truffle oil and top with basil. Serve warm.

SPICY ROSEMARY CASHEWS

MAKES 3½ CUPS

These cashews make an easy and elegant appetizer, party favor, hostess gift or holiday treat.
If you use raw nuts, lightly roast them for 10 to 12 minutes.

1 pound whole unsalted roasted cashews
2 tablespoons minced fresh rosemary
1 teaspoon cayenne pepper

1 teaspoon coarse salt
2 teaspoons dark brown sugar
1 tablespoon butter, melted

Preheat the oven to 350°F. Spread the cashews on a rimmed baking sheet and heat in the oven for 4 to 5 minutes. Combine the remaining ingredients in a medium bowl to form a paste. Add the warm cashews and mix gently until evenly coated. May be served warm or at room temperature.

✎ BRUSCHETTA *and* CROSTINI ✎

What you can put on bruschetta and crostini is limited only by your imagination. Try:

- *Goat cheese with herbs and multi-colored peppercorns*
- *Serrano ham, figs and mint leaves*
- *Chopped sautéed mushrooms and blue cheese*
- *Burrata cheese and prosciutto*
- *Figs and caramelized onion with rosemary*
- *Sun-dried tomato tapenade*
- *Mascarpone cheese topped with sliced strawberries tossed in brown sugar*
- *Melted chocolate, chopped pistachios and chopped dried cherries*

Crostini Tapenade and Classic Bruschetta al Pomodoro, PAGE 66

POMEGRANATE MARTINI

SERVES 4

This pretty, red martini is festive enough for any occasion.

1½ cups pomegranate juice
2 ounces lemon-flavored vodka
1 ounce Cointreau® or other orange liqueur

sparkling water (optional)
pomegranate seeds (if available)
lemon twists

Shake the juice, vodka and Cointreau over ice in an extra-large cocktail shaker and strain into chilled martini glasses. Finish each martini with a splash of sparkling water, pomegranate seeds and a lemon twist.

LYCHEE MARTINI

SERVES 1

Try this exotic cocktail in a glass rimmed with crushed crystallized ginger.

3 ounces premium vodka
1 ounce lychee liqueur
½ ounce Grand Marnier®

ice
1 lychee, peeled and pitted

Shake together the vodka, liqueur and Grand Marnier over ice, and strain into a chilled martini glass. Garnish with the lychee and serve.

FRENCH MARTINI

SERVES 2

Chambord®, a French liqueur dating back to 1685, gives this cocktail a hint of black raspberries.

2 ounces chilled vodka
2 ounces pineapple juice

⅔ ounce Chambord®
juice of 1 lime, plus curled zest

Pour the vodka, juice and Chambord over ice in a cocktail shaker. Shake vigorously to produce a frothy head and strain into chilled martini glasses. Serve straight up with a lime curl.

CHOCOLATE MARTINI

SERVES 2

This chocolate martini is a richly decadent, indulgent treat.

white chocolate shavings, finely chopped
milk chocolate shavings, finely chopped
orange wedges
1 ounce chocolate liqueur

1 ounce white chocolate liqueur
1 ounce vanilla vodka
1 ounce chocolate vodka
1 ounce crème de cacao

Combine the chocolate shavings in a shallow dish. Wet the rims of chilled martini glasses with an orange wedge and dip in the chocolate shavings to coat. Pour the chocolate liqueur and the remaining ingredients over ice in a cocktail shaker. Shake until cold and strain into the prepared glasses.

CAIPIRINHA

SERVES 1

Pronounced "kie-puh-reen-ya," caipirinha is a classic Brazilian cocktail
made with lime and a sugarcane brandy called Cachaça.

1 lime or 3 Key limes, cut into wedges
2 tablespoons sugar
2 to 2½ ounces Cachaça

Gently mash lime wedges in a cocktail glass. Add the sugar and a dash of Cachaça, and muddle until the sugar is mostly dissolved; add crushed ice. Pour in the additional Cachaça, stir and serve.

T'AFIA RATAFIA

COURTESY *of* EXECUTIVE CHEF/OWNER MONICA POPE, T'AFIA

MAKES 4 CUPS

According to Monica Pope, this ratafia "perfectly captures a moment in time, a season at its ripeness, a mouthful of memories."
It can be made with fruit (apples, plums, nectarines, quinces, peaches, cherries, berries, oranges, lemons);
vegetables (carrots, beets, rhubarb); and/or herbs (mint, thyme, rosemary, basil).

seasonal fruit or vegetables, cut open (about 1 cup), and/or crushed herbs
¼ cup organic sugar
¼ organic whole vanilla bean, split

¼ cup Tito's® vodka or any clean-tasting vodka, room temperature
1 bottle crisp white wine, room temperature

This recipe requires advance preparation. In a 2-quart container, mix together the ingredients until the sugar is dissolved. Cover and refrigerate for 3 to 4 weeks. (The ratafia can be made faster by using the juice of the fruit or vegetable instead of the cut fruit.) Strain and discard the solids to serve. Serve shaken or on the rocks as an apéritif.

EL DIABLO

SERVES 1

Contrary to its name, this drink is divine.

2 ounces tequila
¾ ounce crème de cassis (black currant liqueur)

ginger ale
1 lime, quartered

Stir the tequila and crème de cassis over ice in a tall chilled glass. Fill the remainder of the glass with ginger ale and squeeze in the juice of 1 lime wedge. Drop the lime into the glass as a garnish.

ROSÉ WINE FREEZES

SERVES 4

Substitute margarita mix for strawberry daiquiri mix to make this drink a little tangier,
and rim frosted glasses with pastel pink sugar for a pretty presentation.

6 ounces frozen limeade concentrate, thawed
6 ounces frozen strawberry daiquiri mix, thawed
6 ounces rosé wine

6 ounces club soda
1 lime, cut into wedges
sugar

Combine the liquid ingredients in a blender and fill with ice; blend until slushy. Rub the rims of martini glasses with the lime and dip in sugar. Pour and serve immediately.

CHAMPAGNE POMEGRANATE PUNCH

SERVES A CROWD

This bubbly pink punch is perfect for a luncheon, shower or any special occasion.

3 liters ginger ale, divided
½ cup brandy
1 cup pomegranate juice

1 cup peach schnapps
3 bottles brut Champagne or sparkling wine

This recipe requires advance preparation. The night before or at least 6 hours prior to serving, make ice cubes or an ice ring by pouring 1 liter of ginger ale into the desired container and freezing. Pour the brandy, pomegranate juice and schnapps into a large punch bowl. Just prior to serving, gently add the Champagne and the remaining 2 liters of ginger ale. Float the prepared ice cubes or ring in the bowl.

PEACH CHAMPAGNE PUNCH

SERVES A CROWD

This timeless punch is ideal for garden parties, showers and picnics.
Whole mint leaves make a beautiful garnish. Leave out the Champagne for a non-alcoholic alternative.

6 fresh ripe peaches, pitted and chopped (about 3 cups)
1 package (3 ounces) peach-flavored gelatin
12 ounces frozen lemonade concentrate (or limeade)
64 ounces pineapple juice, chilled

3 tablespoons almond extract
1 liter (about 34 ounces) lemon-lime soda, chilled
1 bottle Champagne, chilled

This recipe requires advance preparation. To make the peach ice ring, evenly distribute the chopped peaches in the bottom of a Bundt® pan. Fill with 4 to 5 cups of water and freeze until solid, about 5 to 6 hours or overnight. Bring 1 cup of water to a boil in a large saucepan; remove from heat and whisk in the gelatin until dissolved. Mix in the lemonade, pineapple juice and almond extract. Pour into a punch bowl. When ready to serve, stir in the soda and Champagne. Gently float the prepared ice ring in the punch.

HOLIDAY COFFEE

SERVES 4

A warm, minty treat for a winter's evening,
this coffee is a well-deserved reward for a busy day of holiday preparations.

¾ cup (6 ounces) peppermint schnapps
½ cup (4 ounces) crème de cacao
8 cups hot, strong coffee

½ cup heavy whipping cream
½ cup crushed peppermint sticks

Stir together the schnapps, crème de cacao and coffee in a carafe. Whisk the cream in a small chilled bowl until slightly thickened. Pour the coffee mixture into coffee glasses or mugs, top with the cream and sprinkle with peppermint. Serve immediately.

WHITE WINE SANGRIA

SERVES 8 to 10

This sangria is perfect for sipping slowly on languid days.

2 bottles dry white wine
½ cup sugar
2 lemons, sliced
2 limes, sliced

4 oranges, sliced
1 bunch red grapes
1 cup lemon-lime soda, chilled

This recipe requires advance preparation. Pour the wine and sugar into a large pitcher. Add the lemons, limes and oranges one slice at a time, muddling with a wooden spoon to release the juices. Stir in the grapes and refrigerate several hours or overnight. Add the lemon-lime soda just before serving. Serve over ice, adding fruit to each glass.

OCEAN BREEZE COCKTAIL

SERVES 8

Tropical flavors blend deliciously in this refreshing summer cocktail.

½ cup light brown sugar
½ cup water
½ cup packed fresh mint leaves, plus additional for garnish
1½ cups freshly squeezed orange juice
¾ cup fresh lime juice

5 ounces clear rum
1 orange, halved crosswise and thinly sliced
1 lime, thinly sliced

Bring the brown sugar and water to a boil in a small saucepan over medium-high heat, stirring once. Remove from heat and stir in the mint. Cover and steep for 10 minutes. Strain the liquid into a bowl and discard the mint. Let cool. In a pitcher, combine the prepared syrup with the orange and lime juices and the rum. Divide the orange and lime slices among 8 glasses and fill with ice. Pour the cocktail into the glasses and garnish with mint sprigs.

GINGER MARGARITA

COURTESY *of* ROBERT DEL GRANDE CHEF, CAFE ANNIE, *and* PARTNER, THE GROVE

SERVES 1

Ginger and Thai chiles are unexpected additions to this classic on-the-rocks cocktail.
To intensify the flavor of the aromatic ginger, grate and muddle it with sugar.

2 ounces Herradura® Silver Tequila or other
  high quality silver tequila
1 ounce Cointreau®
1 ounce fresh lime juice
¼ teaspoon minced fresh ginger

pinch of sugar
pinch of minced fresh red Thai chiles
lime wedge

Combine the ingredients, except the lime wedge, with ice in a cocktail shaker. Shake vigorously. Rub the rim of a cocktail glass with lime. Dip the rim in salt. Fill the glass with ice. Decant the shaken ginger margarita over the ice. Garnish with a lime wedge.

THE CHEESE BOARD
COURTESY *of* CENTRAL MARKET

A cheese board to start or finish a meal, or paired with wine as a main event, is a delicious, easy and unique way to connect with friends over food. A selection of cheeses can be assembled to fit almost any menu and there is an almost overwhelming variety from which to choose. To simplify choices and present an interesting assortment, develop a theme for a cheese board just as you might develop a theme for a wine-tasting: select the offerings by region of origin, by type or by maker.

General Tips
- Five different cheeses is a good minimum for an interesting assortment (taste, color, texture); include one triple crème, one hard, one blue, one goat and one mild semisoft.
- Allowing cheese to come to room temperature brings out the full flavor and makes it easier to handle.
- Slice cheese just before serving (to keep it from drying out).
- Plan on 2 ounces of cheese per person as part of an appetizer or dessert, or 4 to 6 ounces if cheese is the focus.

Tools
- Use rustic boards, marble slabs or wicker trays as serving platters; they emphasize the artisan origins of many cheeses.
- Different cheeses require different knives: knives with holes keep soft cheeses from sticking to the blade; rectangular cheese knives (cleavers) and pointed knives are good for slicing hard cheeses; narrow blades are best for semifirm cheeses or for spreading softer cheeses; wide blades are good for crumbly, soft cheese or for making cubes of firm cheese. Use a different knife for each cheese to keep flavors from intermingling.

Accompaniments and Presentation
- To turn a cheese course into a more substantial antipasti plate, add cured meats, olives and marinated vegetables (blend with your theme or region).
- Serve the cheese board with an assortment of quality breads and crackers (avoid overly salty crackers); a French baguette is always good, but experiment—more flavorful breads with robust cheeses such as cheddar, or raisin pecan bread with blue cheese.
- For added flavor and texture, include honeycomb, quince paste, mustard, jam or herbs.
- To add color and to complement the saltiness of the cheeses, add sweet fresh fruits like apples, grapes, figs and pears, or dried fruits like Medjool dates, apricots and cherries.
- As a final touch, scatter your cheese platter with nuts such as pistachios, Marcona almonds or spiced pecans.

73

❧ REGIONAL CHEESE, WINE *and* ACCOMPANIMENTS ❧

American "New England"
- *Five-cheese regional sampler: Westfield Farm Plain Capri; Boggy Meadow Farm Raw Milk Swiss; Grafton Classic White Cheddar 4 year; Smith's Smoked Gouda; Great Hill Blue*
- *Wines: Chardonnay, Zinfandel and Sauvignon Blanc*
- *Accompaniments: Green apples, dried cranberries and cherries, spiced pecans, wheat and water crackers*

Spanish
- *Five-cheese regional sampler: Mahon; La Serena; Manchego Monte Alba 1 year; Roncal; Cabrales*
- *Wines: Amontillado sherry, Rioja, Albariño or Verdejo*
- *Accompaniments: Flatbread, crackers, honey, Marcona almonds, quince, Seville orange marmalade, figs and dates*

French
- *Five-cheese regional sampler: Chabichou du Poitou; Chaource; Comte 12 month; Epoisses; Roquefort Baragnaudes*
- *Wines: Red or white Bordeaux, Champagne and Chablis*
- *Accompaniments: Sliced French baguette, pâté, pears, grapes and toasted hazelnuts*

soups, sandwi

ches and more

menu sampler

READY *and* WAITING

Warm Spinach and
Roasted Red Pepper Sandwich

Roasted Balsamic Tomato Soup

Any Day Chocolate Cake

HOT DINNER *on a*
COLD NIGHT

Moroccan Vegetable Stew

Grilled Lamb Burger Pitas
with Tzatziki Sauce

Mâche and Fig Salad

Pumpkin Bread Pudding

GIRLS' NIGHT IN

Baked Artichoke Brie Spread

Fragrant Carrot Soup

Grilled Chicken and
Caramelized Onion Sandwiches

Over-the-Top Fudgy Brownies

Avocado Cucumber Soup with Cilantro, PAGE 78

AVOCADO CUCUMBER SOUP *with* CILANTRO

SERVES 6

This elegant chilled soup is great for warm weather entertaining or as part of a luncheon menu.

1½ cups chicken broth
2 large cucumbers, peeled and chopped (about 2½ cups)
2 avocados, pitted, peeled and chopped
1 medium sweet onion, chopped (about 1½ cups)
½ cup fresh lime juice

1 cup loosely packed fresh cilantro leaves, plus additional
½ to 1 fresh jalapeño, seeded and coarsely chopped
½ teaspoon ground cumin
½ teaspoon coarse salt
plain yogurt (or sour cream)

This recipe requires advance preparation. Purée the ingredients except yogurt in a blender until smooth. Refrigerate for at least 3 hours or up to 1 day. Ladle into bowls, top with a dollop of yogurt and garnish with cilantro. Serve chilled.

WHITE GAZPACHO

MAKES 6 CUPS

A refreshingly cool start to any meal, this gazpacho is less well known than its tomato-based twin but equally delicious.
Substitute low-fat sour cream or plain yogurt for a lighter version.

3 cucumbers, peeled and roughly chopped
1 clove garlic, minced
2 cups chicken broth
2 cups sour cream
3 tablespoons white vinegar

1 teaspoon coarse salt
½ teaspoon white pepper
chopped tomatoes
snipped fresh chives

This recipe requires advance preparation. Place the cucumbers, garlic and broth into a blender and purée. In a large bowl, combine the sour cream, vinegar, salt and white pepper. Add the cucumber mixture to the sour cream mixture and stir well. Chill for several hours. Top each serving with chopped tomatoes and chives. Served chilled.

ROASTED BALSAMIC TOMATO SOUP

SERVES 8

Get the taste of fresh summer tomatoes all year long with this tangy twist on classic tomato soup.
Look for good quality canned Italian tomatoes; diced can be substituted for whole, but crushed tomatoes do not have the same full flavor.

2 cups beef broth, divided
2 tablespoons loosely packed brown sugar
6 tablespoons Balsamic vinegar
2 tablespoons soy sauce
2 cups chopped onion

8 garlic cloves
4 28-ounce cans whole tomatoes, drained
1½ cups half-and-half
freshly ground pepper
fresh basil chiffonade

Preheat the oven to 500°F. Combine 1 cup of the broth, the sugar, vinegar and soy sauce in a small bowl. Lightly oil two 9 by 13-inch baking dishes. Divide the onions, garlic and tomatoes between the prepared dishes. Pour the broth mixture evenly over the tomatoes and bake for 50 minutes or until lightly browned. Pour the remaining cup of broth and the half-and-half over the roasted tomatoes, dividing equally between the dishes. Allow to cool sightly. Working in batches, purée the tomato mixture in a blender until smooth. Strain the mixture through a sieve into a stockpot, discarding the solids. Heat gently over medium. Finish with pepper and basil.

ITALIAN WEDDING SOUP

SERVES 6 *to* 8

Italian Wedding Soup is a traditional Italian-American soup that "marries" green vegetables and meats.
The meatballs can be made in advance and refrigerated on a baking sheet until you are ready to brown them.

Meatballs:
2 slices hearty white sandwich bread, torn into pieces
½ cup milk
1 egg yolk
½ cup freshly grated Parmesan cheese
3 tablespoons chopped fresh parsley
3 cloves garlic, minced
¾ teaspoon coarse salt
½ teaspoon freshly ground pepper
½ teaspoon dried oregano
½ pound ground beef
½ pound ground pork
2 tablespoons extra virgin olive oil

Soup:
1 tablespoon extra virgin olive oil
2 cloves garlic, minced
¼ teaspoon crushed red pepper
96 ounces (3 quarts) chicken broth
1 large head kale or Swiss chard, stemmed, leaves chopped
1 cup orzo pasta
3 tablespoons chopped fresh parsley
coarse salt and freshly ground pepper
freshly grated Parmesan cheese

Using a potato masher, mash together the bread and milk in a large bowl until smooth. Add the remaining meatball ingredients, except for the beef, pork and olive oil, and mash to combine. Add the meat and knead by hand until well combined. Form into meatballs (should yield about 55 small or 30 larger meatballs) and arrange on a rimmed baking sheet. Cover with plastic wrap and refrigerate until firm, at least 30 minutes. Heat the olive oil in a large saucepan and sauté the meatballs in batches until lightly browned but not cooked through. Remove with a slotted spoon and set aside. Heat 1 tablespoon of olive oil in a Dutch oven or large stockpot over medium-high. Sauté the garlic and red pepper until fragrant, about 30 seconds. Add the broth and bring to a boil. Stir in the kale and simmer until softened, about 10 to 15 minutes. Stir in the meatballs and orzo, reduce heat to medium and simmer until the meatballs are cooked through and the orzo is tender, about 15 minutes. Stir in the parsley and season with salt and pepper. Ladle into bowls, top with cheese and serve immediately.

SOUTHWESTERN CHICKEN SOUP

SERVES 6

This chunky, homestyle soup is full of the flavors of the Southwest. It makes a simple, satisfying weeknight staple.

3 boneless skinless chicken breast halves
3 slices bacon, cut into 1-inch pieces
2 white potatoes, peeled and cubed
5 cups chicken stock (reserved from cooking chicken)
1 cup prepared Pace® Picante Sauce
½ cup chopped onion
1 teaspoon coarse salt

4½ ounces canned chopped green chiles
2 green onions, chopped
1 ear fresh corn, kernels cut from cob
crushed tortilla chips
1 cup shredded sharp cheddar cheese
2 avocados, pitted, peeled and chopped

Place the chicken in a stockpot and fill with enough water to cover, at least 6 cups (so you have enough for stock). Bring to a simmer over medium heat, cover and cook for 15 to 20 minutes. Remove the chicken from the pot; reserve 5 cups of the stock and set aside. Let the chicken cool slightly and chop into bite-size pieces. Brown the bacon in the empty stockpot over medium-high heat. Add the potato cubes and stir until coated with the bacon drippings. Add the reserved chicken stock, picante sauce, onions and salt. Simmer, stirring occasionally, over medium-low heat for 45 minutes to 1 hour or until the potatoes are tender. Stir in the green chiles, green onions, corn and chicken, and heat through. Add crushed tortilla chips to soup bowls, ladle in the soup, and top with the cheese and avocado.

FRAGRANT CARROT SOUP

SERVES 8 *to* 10

This aromatic soup uses only a little cream; it gets most of its creamy texture from the puréed vegetables.
An immersion blender may be used to purée this soup easily in the stockpot.

5 to 7 cups vegetable broth
1 tablespoon olive oil
1 medium onion, thinly sliced
2½ teaspoons coarse salt, divided
2 cloves garlic, minced
1½ teaspoons cumin seed, toasted and ground
1 teaspoon coriander seed, toasted and ground

3 teaspoons peeled and grated fresh ginger
pinch of cayenne pepper
2 pounds carrots, peeled and thinly sliced
1 medium sweet potato, peeled and thinly sliced
½ cup freshly squeezed orange juice
3 tablespoons chopped fresh cilantro
½ cup heavy whipping cream

Heat the broth in a saucepan over low. Heat the olive oil in a stockpot; add the onions and ½ teaspoon of the salt. Sauté for 5 minutes then add the garlic, cumin, coriander, ginger and cayenne. Cook until the onions are soft, about 10 minutes. Add a little of the warm broth if the mixture dries out. Add the carrots, sweet potatoes, 1 more teaspoon of the salt and 4 cups of the warmed broth. Bring to a boil, reduce heat and simmer until the carrots are tender. Allow to cool slightly. Purée the soup in small batches in a blender. Return the soup to the pot and add the orange juice and additional broth to achieve desired consistency. Season again with the remaining teaspoon of salt and additional cayenne if desired. In a small bowl, stir together the cilantro and cream. Serve the soup with a drizzle of the cilantro cream on top.

> ### ❧ WHOLE SPICES ☙
>
> *To toast and grind whole spices like cumin and coriander seeds, place the seeds in a small dry skillet over low heat. Shake the pan and stir the seeds until they release their aroma and darken slightly, about 1 to 2 minutes. Grind the cooled seeds in a grinder, or use a mortar and pestle.*

80

PUMPKIN MUSHROOM SOUP

SERVES 4

A just right combination of sweet and savory, this is a velvety, delicious soup.
You can use any assortment of your favorite mushrooms in place of the cremini.

4 tablespoons (½ stick) butter
½ pound cremini mushrooms, thinly sliced
½ cup chopped onion
2 tablespoons all-purpose flour
1 tablespoon curry powder
3 cups chicken broth

15 ounces canned pure pumpkin purée
2 tablespoons honey
dash of nutmeg
1 teaspoon coarse salt
½ teaspoon freshly ground pepper
2 cups (1 pint) half-and-half

Melt the butter in a stockpot over medium heat; add the mushrooms and onions, and sauté for 10 minutes. Stir in the flour and curry; add the broth and stir for 1 minute. Add the pumpkin, honey and seasonings, and mix well. Stir over medium-high heat until the soup comes to a simmer. Reduce heat and continue to simmer for 10 minutes, stirring occasionally. Add the half-and-half and heat through without boiling. Serve immediately.

Fragrant Carrot Soup, PAGE 80

Braised Veal Stew Provençal, PAGE 83

BRAISED VEAL STEW PROVENÇAL

SERVES 4 *to* 6

This rustic stew is one of those dishes that is just as good the next day.
Cool it to room temperature, cover and chill overnight; reheat over low to serve.

¼ cup olive oil
2 pounds boneless veal shoulder, cut into 1½-inch pieces
coarse salt and freshly ground pepper
3 onions, chopped
3 large cloves garlic, minced, divided
28 ounces canned plum tomatoes, including juice
½ pound carrots, peeled and cut into 3 by ½-inch sticks

4 strips orange peel, julienned
1 cup dry white wine
¾ teaspoon dried thyme
¾ teaspoon dried rosemary
½ pound pearl onions, peeled
½ cup oil-cured black olives, seeded and chopped

Preheat the oven to 325°F. In a large Dutch oven, heat the olive oil over medium. Add the veal, season with salt and pepper, and brown lightly. Remove the veal and reduce heat to medium-low. Add the onions and 2 cloves of garlic, and sauté until softened. Stir in the tomatoes and carrots, and cook for 5 minutes. Add the veal back to the pan and add the orange peel, wine, thyme and rosemary. Cover and braise in the oven for 1½ hours. Meanwhile, bring a large saucepan of water to a boil. Cut an "X" in the stems of the pearl onions to keep them whole. Boil the onions for 20 minutes; drain and set aside. Remove the veal from the oven. Stir in the pearl onions and remaining clove of garlic, and season with salt and pepper. Serve topped with the olives.

CHICKEN BOUILLABAISSE *with* GARLICKY BEANS

SERVES 6

Made with chicken, this is an interesting update of the traditional seafood-based bouillabaisse.
The garlicky beans also make a great stand-alone appetizer or side dish.

3 tablespoons olive oil
1 large onion, thinly sliced
1 teaspoon dried thyme
¼ teaspoon saffron threads
2 4-inch long strips orange peel (orange part only)
¾ cup dry white wine
14½ ounces canned diced tomatoes, undrained
14 ounces chicken broth
6 chicken leg quarters (drumsticks and thighs),
    skin removed

12 ½-inch thick baguette slices,
    brushed with olive oil and toasted

Rouille:
½ cup mayonnaise
2 cloves garlic, minced
2 teaspoons fresh lemon juice
½ teaspoon paprika
coarse salt and freshly ground pepper

Garlicky Beans:
30 ounces canned garbanzo beans, rinsed and drained
2 tablespoons olive oil
2 cloves garlic, minced
dash of cayenne pepper
½ cup chopped fresh mint
1 cup crumbled feta cheese

Preheat the oven to 375°F. Heat the olive oil in a large Dutch oven over medium-high. Sauté the onions until soft and golden, about 8 minutes. Add the thyme, saffron, orange peel and wine; bring to a boil. Add the tomatoes and broth, and return to a boil. Add the chicken in a single layer, submerging it in the sauce; return to a boil. Cover and place in the oven. Bake until the chicken is cooked through and very tender, about 45 to 50 minutes. Meanwhile, combine the mayonnaise, garlic, lemon juice and paprika in a small bowl; season with salt and pepper, and set aside. Remove the chicken from the oven and keep covered. Maintain the oven temperature at 375°F. Lightly oil an oval baking dish. Mix the beans with the olive oil, garlic and cayenne in the prepared dish. Bake for 12 minutes. Remove the beans from the oven and stir in the mint and cheese. Divide the chicken and sauce among six shallow bowls. Top each serving with 2 toasted baguette slices. Finish with a dollop of the rouille and a spoonful of the beans.

TUSCAN LENTIL SOUP

SERVES 8

Lentils make for a hearty, nutritious soup that is especially delicious on cool nights.
To make this soup spicier, use hot Italian sausage in place of the sweet.

16 ounces dried brown lentils
3 tablespoons garlic-infused olive oil
1¼ pounds sweet Italian sausage, casings removed and
   formed into ½-inch balls
1 medium onion, diced
2 stalks celery, diced
1 carrot, peeled and grated

4 cloves garlic, minced
8 cups beef broth
½ teaspoon coarse salt
½ teaspoon fennel seed
crushed red pepper
freshly ground pepper
1 ounce dry sherry (about 2 tablespoons)

Rinse and sort through the lentils. Heat the olive oil in a stockpot over medium. Add the sausage, vegetables and garlic, and cook until the vegetables are tender and the meatballs are browned on all sides. Add the lentils, broth and seasonings; bring to a boil. Reduce heat, cover and simmer until the lentils are tender and the soup thickens, about 1 to 1½ hours. Add hot water in small amounts if the soup is too thick. Ladle into bowls and drizzle with sherry before serving.

BUTTERNUT SQUASH BISQUE *with* FRIED SAGE

SERVES 4 *to* 6

This squash soup is a rich autumn treat with a pretty finish of chopped pecans and fried sage.

5 tablespoons unsalted butter, divided
2 medium leeks, white parts only,
   washed well and coarsely chopped
1 cup coarsely chopped celery stalks and leaves
2 carrots, peeled and coarsely chopped
1 tablespoon peeled and chopped fresh ginger
½ to 1 fresh jalapeño, seeded and coarsely chopped

2 pounds butternut squash, peeled,
   seeded and cut into cubes
4 cups chicken broth
½ cup half-and-half
coarse salt and ground white pepper
12 fresh sage leaves
½ cup chopped pecans, toasted

Melt 4 tablespoons of the butter in a stockpot over medium heat. Add the leeks, celery, carrots, ginger and jalapeño, and sauté approximately 15 minutes or until wilted. Stir in the squash and broth, and bring to a boil. Reduce heat to medium-low, cover and simmer 20 to 30 minutes or until all of the vegetables are very soft. Allow to cool slightly. Working in 4 or 5 batches, purée in a food processor or blender until smooth. Return the soup to the pot and stir in the half-and-half. Heat through but do not allow to boil as the half-and-half might curdle. Season with salt and white pepper. To fry the sage, melt the remaining tablespoon of butter in a large skillet. Add the sage leaves and cook over medium heat, turning once, until crisp. Transfer to paper towels to drain. To serve, ladle the bisque into bowls and garnish with the sage and pecans.

> ✂ LEEKS ✎
>
> *Leeks are in the same family as onions but have a mild, almost sweet flavor. Cut off ¼ inch of the root and most but not all of the green tops. Chop leeks before washing or soaking them to make sure you remove all of the grit.*

MOROCCAN VEGETABLE STEW

SERVES 6 to 8

Let a slow cooker do all the work. Serve this exotic stew as a starter or as a vegetarian meal with matlouh
or other flatbread (ideal for dipping into the savory sauce).

2 tablespoons olive oil
3 cloves garlic, minced
1 teaspoon dried coriander
1 teaspoon dried cumin
½ teaspoon cayenne pepper
¼ teaspoon cinnamon
5 cups vegetable broth
2½ cups diced eggplant, about 2 medium
2 cups peeled and sliced carrots, about 5 small

2 cups cauliflower florets, about one small head
2 cups sliced zucchini, about 2 medium
1 cup chopped onion, about 1 medium
29 ounces canned stewed tomatoes
15 ounces canned garbanzo beans
1 cup chopped roasted almonds
¾ cup currants
1 tablespoon coarse salt
½ cup non-fat plain yogurt (optional)

Heat the olive oil in a medium sauté pan over medium-low. Add the garlic and spices and cook until fragrant, about 1 to 2 minutes; be careful not to burn the garlic. Scrape the garlic and spices into a slow cooker. Add the broth and the remaining ingredients (except the yogurt) and stir. Cook on high for 6 to 7 hours. Allow to cool slightly. Purée 3 cups of the stew in a blender or food processor and return to the slow cooker, stirring to combine. Serve warm with a dollop of yogurt, if desired.

GRILLED CHICKEN *and* CARAMELIZED ONION SANDWICHES

SERVES 2 to 3

Caramelized onions, raisins and pesto take the familiar grilled chicken sandwich to a different level.
Wrap the sandwich tightly in parchment paper and tape, then slice it. This is a great tip for keeping any stacked sandwich neat.

85

2 tablespoons olive oil, divided
1 yellow onion, sliced
2 tablespoons brown sugar
1 tablespoon Balsamic vinegar
4 tablespoons raisins, soaked in hot water until plump
2 boneless skinless chicken breast halves, pounded

coarse salt and freshly ground pepper
2 to 3 crusty sandwich rolls
2 vine-ripened tomatoes, thinly sliced
several leaves red or green leaf lettuce
2 tablespoons pesto

Preheat the grill. Heat 1 tablespoon of the olive oil in a medium skillet over medium. Add the onions and gently sauté for 20 minutes or until softened. Add the brown sugar and vinegar, and cook for 10 more minutes. While the onions are cooking, coat the chicken breasts in the remaining tablespoon of olive oil and season with salt and pepper. Grill the chicken for 3 to 4 minutes on each side or until cooked through. Drain the raisins and add to the onions; gently stir and remove from heat. Slice the rolls in half lengthwise and remove some of the soft bread inside to make a shallow well in each piece. Layer the bottom halves with the chicken, caramelized onions, tomatoes and lettuce. Spread the tops with pesto and press the halves together.

ASIAN CHICKEN WRAPS

Lunch is all wrapped up with these easy to make, fun to eat sandwiches.
Serve them with steamed edamame for a complete meal.

1 tablespoon sesame oil
½ teaspoon crushed red pepper
1 large clove garlic, minced
1 teaspoon peeled and grated fresh ginger
2 pounds boneless skinless chicken breast halves,
   cut into ½-inch strips
1 lime

8 to 10 white or whole wheat flour tortillas
½ cup prepared hoisin sauce
3 to 4 green onions, chopped
½ bunch green leaf lettuce, chopped
1 cup chopped fresh cilantro
1 cup peeled and grated cucumber

Heat the oil, red pepper and garlic in a large skillet over medium. Add the ginger and chicken. Sauté until cooked through and the juices run clear, about 5 to 7 minutes. Squeeze the lime over the cooked chicken and remove from heat. Warm the tortillas one at a time in a skillet. Top each tortilla with hoisin sauce, green onions, chicken, lettuce, cilantro and cucumber, and roll tightly. Secure the wraps with toothpicks and slice on the diagonal to serve.

TURKEY, SPINACH, BLUE CHEESE *and* CRANBERRY WRAPS

MAKES 8 WRAPS

These wraps are a light and lovely way to serve holiday leftovers, or to
capture the flavors of Thanksgiving anytime of the year.

86

8 ounces cream cheese, softened
1½ tablespoons buttermilk
1 clove garlic, minced
1 tablespoon minced onion
4 ounces (½ cup) crumbled blue cheese
½ cup chopped pecans, toasted
¾ cup dried cranberries, coarsely chopped

8 (8-inch) flour tortillas
8 slices roasted turkey breast
½ cup prepared roasted raspberry chipotle sauce
1 to 2 medium Granny Smith apples, cored and thinly sliced
2 medium carrots, peeled and shredded
3 cups fresh baby spinach

Combine the cream cheese, buttermilk, garlic and onion in a medium bowl. Add the blue cheese, pecans and cranberries and stir to combine. Spread the mixture evenly over each tortilla; layer with the turkey, chipotle sauce, apple slices, shredded carrots and spinach. Roll each tortilla tightly and use toothpicks to secure. Cover with plastic wrap and refrigerate up to 4 hours. Slice on the diagonal to serve.

Turkey, Spinach, Blue Cheese and Cranberry Wraps, PAGE 86

Grilled Lamb Burger Pitas with Tzatziki Sauce, PAGE 89

GRILLED LAMB BURGER PITAS *with* TZATZIKI SAUCE

SERVES 5

This sandwich, made with ground rather than rotisserie lamb, is a make-at-home version of the classic Greek gyro.
Try serving it with a side of the Greek Quinoa Salad (page 120). The tzatziki sauce is also great served on its own as a dip with pita chips.

Tzatziki Sauce:
1 cucumber, peeled and diced
7 ounces Greek yogurt
1 clove garlic, minced
1 teaspoon chopped fresh dill
1 tablespoon fresh lemon juice

Burgers:
2 pounds ground lamb
2 tablespoons Worcestershire sauce
2 teaspoons Turkish or Greek seasoning
1 medium onion, cut into ¼-inch slices
olive oil
5 whole pitas, halved
3 tomatoes, thickly sliced and halved

Pat the cucumbers dry and set aside. Combine the remaining sauce ingredients and mix well. Fold in the cucumbers and chill. Heat the grill to medium-high. Combine the lamb, Worcestershire and seasoning in a medium bowl. Form into mini burgers about 1½ inches in diameter, making about 20 burgers. Lightly brush both sides of the onion slices with olive oil. Grill the burgers and onion slices for 2 to 3 minutes on each side. Fill each pita half with 2 mini lamb burgers, grilled onions, tomatoes and *Tzatziki Sauce*.

PEPPER JACK TURKEY BURGERS *with* JICAMA SLAW

SERVES 8

The jicama slaw gives these burgers a crunch and a kick.
Jicama can be hard to peel with a vegetable peeler; instead cut off the ends and use a paring knife to remove the outer layer.

Jicama Slaw:
2 tablespoons rice wine vinegar
2 tablespoons olive oil
cayenne pepper
dash of sugar
coarse salt and freshly ground pepper
2 cups peeled and thinly sliced jicama
1 cup thinly sliced cabbage
1 carrot, thinly sliced
3 tablespoons snipped fresh chives
2 jalapeños, seeded and minced

Burgers:
2 pounds ground turkey
1 medium white onion, diced
2 tablespoons soy sauce
2 tablespoons ketchup
3 cloves garlic, minced
¼ teaspoon freshly ground pepper
1 cup shredded pepper jack cheese
8 whole wheat buns
8 slices bacon, cooked until crisp
1 avocado, pitted, peeled and sliced

Whisk together the vinegar, olive oil, cayenne and sugar in a small bowl; season with salt and pepper. In a large bowl, combine the vegetables, add the vinaigrette and toss to coat. Chill for 1 to 2 hours before serving.

Combine the turkey, onions, soy sauce, ketchup, garlic and pepper in a large bowl. Mix in the cheese and form into 8 patties. Heat a grill or a skillet coated with nonstick cooking spray. Add the burgers and cook for about 6 to 8 minutes on each side. Serve the burgers on the buns topped with *Jicama Slaw*, bacon and avocado.

BUFFALO MUSHROOM BURGERS

SERVES 4

This "black tie" burger gets its elegance from mushrooms and onions sautéed in white wine.
Complete the meal with sliced melon and Rosemary Sweet Potato Wedges (recipe below).

1 pound ground buffalo or bison meat
4 tablespoons minced onion, divided
1 tablespoon chopped fresh parsley
1 tablespoon Worcestershire sauce
1 teaspoon chopped fresh sage
½ teaspoon coarse salt, plus additional
¼ teaspoon freshly ground pepper, plus additional
2 teaspoons peanut oil

2 teaspoons butter, plus additional
8 ounces button mushrooms,
    stems removed and caps quartered
2 tablespoons white wine
4 whole wheat hamburger buns
4 slices provolone cheese

Combine the meat, 2 tablespoons of the onion, the parsley, Worcestershire, sage, salt and pepper; shape into 4 patties. Heat the oil and butter together in a skillet over medium-high. Add the patties and cook, turning once, until brown on both sides and cooked through. Remove the burgers and set aside. Combine the mushrooms and the remaining 2 tablespoons of onion in the same skillet, and sauté for 4 to 5 minutes. Add the wine and bring to a simmer; reduce heat to low. Return the burgers to the skillet, cover and let cook for 2 to 3 minutes or until heated through. Season with salt and pepper. Lightly spread the buns with butter and toast in a skillet or under a broiler. Serve the patties on a toasted bun topped with the provolone and the mushroom mixture.

☙ ROSEMARY SWEET POTATO WEDGES ☙
SERVES 4

3 medium sweet potatoes
2 tablespoons olive oil
1 teaspoon minced fresh rosemary leaves
coarse salt and freshly ground pepper

Preheat the oven to 400°F. Cut the potatoes into small to medium-size wedges. Place the potatoes on a large baking pan, drizzle with the olive oil and toss to coat. Sprinkle with the rosemary and season with salt and pepper. Roast the potatoes on the middle rack of the oven for 20 minutes or until tender; turn once halfway through the cooking time.

GRILLED PORTOBELLO MUSHROOM BURGERS

SERVES 4

Marinating and grilling portobello mushrooms enhances their meaty texture and complex flavor.
For a more rustic sandwich, serve on thickly sliced and toasted sourdough bread instead of a bun.
You can also slice the mushrooms and serve on mini buns for a delicious appetizer.

4 portobello mushroom caps
4 tablespoons Balsamic vinegar
1½ to 2 tablespoons olive oil, plus additional
1 large red onion, thickly sliced

4 kaiser rolls or hamburger buns
4 ounces goat cheese
1 large tomato, thickly sliced
coarse salt and freshly ground pepper

Remove the mushroom stems and wipe the caps clean with a paper towel. Marinate the mushroom caps in a resealable plastic bag with the vinegar and olive oil for at least 1 hour. Preheat the grill to medium-high. Lightly brush the onions and buns with olive oil on both sides. Grill the mushroom caps and onions until desired doneness, about 5 minutes, flipping halfway through. Mushrooms should be firm but fork tender. Lightly toast the rolls or buns on the grill. When toasted, spread the insides with the goat cheese. Place the mushrooms, onions and tomatoes on the bottom half of the rolls or buns, season with salt and pepper, top and serve.

BRIE, SERRANO *and* FIG PANINI

SERVES 4

This warm sandwich is a perfect pairing of sweet and salty flavors.
If you do not have a panini press, this sandwich can just as easily be prepared in a skillet.
Cook each side over medium heat for 4 to 6 minutes, using another small heavy skillet to weigh the sandwich down.

1 loaf crusty Italian bread, cut into 8 ½-inch slices
4 tablespoons fig preserves
½ pound Serrano ham, thinly sliced
½ pound Brie, rind removed and softened
extra virgin olive oil

Preheat a panini press (a skillet with a smaller heavy lid as a weight can be substituted). Evenly spread 4 slices of bread with the fig preserves; top with the ham. Spread the Brie on the remaining 4 slices of bread. Close the sandwiches and use a pastry brush to coat the outside of the sandwiches with olive oil. Place the sandwiches on the press one at a time and grill until crispy and golden, about 4 minutes. (It is better to cook a sandwich on lower heat for a longer time, so that the cheese melts and the bread turns crisp and toasty without burning.)

✂ PANINI IDEAS ✄

Try these flavorful combinations or experiment with your own. For a meal that has something for everyone, offer a panini station at your next gathering.

- *Maple ham, crisp green apples and Vermont white cheddar*
- *Olive tapenade, tomato and mozzarella*
- *Roast beef, pear, Gorgonzola and caramelized onions*
- *Mushrooms and Fontina cheese*
- *Grilled chicken, Monterey Jack cheese, poblano pesto and black beans*
- *Peanut butter, honey and bananas (for the kids or the kid in you)*

ROASTED RED PEPPER *and* THREE CHEESE SPREAD

MAKES 1 QUART

Loaded with flavor, this spread breathes new life into the traditional Southern pimento cheese.
It is great spread thin on a tea sandwich, piled high on crusty bread, or served as an appetizer with raw vegetables and hearty crackers.

8 ounces smoked gouda cheese, shredded (2 cups)
8 ounces sharp cheddar cheese, shredded (2 cups)
8 ounces mozzarella cheese, shredded (2 cups)
¾ cup mayonnaise

14 ounces roasted red bell peppers, drained
½ teaspoon cayenne pepper
½ teaspoon dry mustard
1 fresh jalapeño, seeded and chopped

Combine the ingredients in a food processor. Pulse for 1 minute until well combined, scraping down the sides of the bowl as needed. Transfer to a container with a lid and chill until ready to serve.

Steak and Arugula Sandwiches, PAGE 93

TUNA PAN BAGNAT

SERVES 4

Pan bagnat is, quite simply, a Niçoise salad served on bread.
Often served on the beaches of Nice, this sandwich has a taste reminiscent of the Côte d'Azur.

1 loaf crusty French bread
1 clove garlic, halved
4 to 6 ounces oil-packed imported tuna, drained
⅓ cup diced red onion
⅛ cup sliced, pitted black olives,
   such as Niçoise or Kalamata
juice of 1 lemon

¼ teaspoon coarse salt
freshly ground pepper
⅛ cup extra virgin olive oil
¼ cup fresh basil chiffonade
1 tomato, thinly sliced
2 hard-boiled eggs, thinly sliced

∾ LAVENDER LEMONADE ∾
MAKES ABOUT 7 CUPS

2 tablespoons dried lavender buds
1¼ cups fresh lemon juice (about 8 to 10 lemons)
¾ to 1 cup sugar

In a small saucepan, boil the lavender buds in 1 cup of water for 10 minutes, then remove the pot from heat and let it sit for 15 minutes. Strain out the lavender buds and reserve the water. Combine the lemon juice, lavender water and sugar in a 2-quart pitcher. Stir well and add up to 5 cups of cold water as desired; chill. If desired, cut additional lemon slices for garnish.

Slice the bread in half lengthwise and remove some of the soft bread inside. Rub the interior with the garlic. Combine the tuna, red onion, olives, lemon juice, salt and pepper in a medium bowl and stir to combine, breaking up the big chunks of tuna. In a small bowl, whisk together the olive oil and basil. Spoon the tuna mixture onto the bottom half of the bread and layer the tomato and egg slices on top. Drizzle with the basil-olive oil dressing. Press the top half of the bread onto the sandwich and wrap tightly in wax paper or foil. Let the sandwich sit for 15 to 20 minutes before slicing. To serve, use a sharp bread knife to cut into 2-inch sections.

93

STEAK *and* ARUGULA SANDWICHES

SERVES 4

With a big handful of gourmet potato chips, this upscale sandwich is steak and potatoes reinterpreted.

3 filet mignon steaks (about 6 ounces each)
coarse salt and freshly ground pepper
2 cups fresh arugula
1 tablespoon olive oil

4 ciabatta rolls or other crusty bread
6 ounces spreadable garlic and herb cheese such as Boursin®
2 to 3 vine-ripened tomatoes, sliced

Preheat the grill to medium. Season the steaks with salt and pepper. Grill to desired doneness, about 6 minutes per side for rare. Remove from the grill and allow to rest for 5 minutes. Thinly slice the steaks and set aside. In a small bowl, toss the arugula with the olive oil; season with salt and pepper. Slice the rolls and remove some of the soft bread inside to make a shallow well in each piece. Spread the cheese on both sides of the bread. On the bottom layer, place tomato slices and top with the sliced steak and arugula. Add the top half of the bread and press together gently.

ITALIAN STUFFED CIABATTA

SERVES 4 *to* 6

Highlighting favorite flavors from Italy, this rustic ham and cheese is equally satisfying as an appetizer or a meal.

1 loaf ciabatta bread

12 ounces fresh mozzarella, sliced

12 thin slices (3 ounces) prosciutto

½ cup prepared or *Classic Basil Pesto* (recipe below)

Preheat the oven to 350°F. Slice the bread in half lengthwise and remove some of the soft bread inside to make a shallow well in each piece. Press the mozzarella slices onto the bottom half of the bread. Arrange the prosciutto over the mozzarella to cover. Spread the top half of the bread with pesto. Press the bread halves together. Place the sandwich on a baking sheet and warm in the oven for approximately 10 to 15 minutes. Let set for 2 to 3 minutes. Cut into individual servings or slice into small pieces to serve as an appetizer. Serve warm.

CLASSIC BASIL PESTO

SERVES 4 *to* 6

Fresh pesto can be more than a topping for pasta. Try it on a tomato basil sandwich made with crusty Italian bread, ripe heirloom tomatoes and fresh mozzarella cheese—grilled, broiled or pressed.

2 cups firmly packed fresh basil

½ cup pine nuts, toasted

4 cloves garlic, minced

¼ cup extra virgin olive oil

¾ cup freshly grated Parmesan cheese

coarse salt and freshly ground pepper

Combine the basil, pine nuts and garlic in a food processor, and pulse until finely chopped. With the machine running, gradually add the olive oil. Add the cheese and season with salt and pepper. Briefly pulse until the mixture forms a thick paste. Toss with pasta or use as a sandwich spread.

94

WARM SPINACH *and* ROASTED RED PEPPER SANDWICH

SERVES 4 *to* 6

Warm and toasty, this sandwich offers a lot of flavor for very little effort.

1 large loaf crusty Italian bread

6 ounces thinly sliced provolone cheese

3 ounces fresh baby spinach

2 tablespoons Balsamic vinegar

1 tablespoon olive oil

coarse salt and freshly ground pepper

5 ounces whole roasted red bell peppers, drained

Preheat the oven to 350°F. Cut the bread in half horizontally on a large cutting board. Cover the bottom half with the cheese, followed by the spinach. Drizzle with the vinegar and olive oil, season with salt and pepper, and top with the peppers. Close the sandwich, wrap in foil and bake until warm, about 15 minutes. Serve immediately.

MUSHROOM QUICHE

SERVES 8

A traditional French dish, quiches are typically made with eggs and milk or cream baked in a pie crust.
This savory version will melt in your mouth at breakfast, lunch or dinner.

1 refrigerated pie crust, unbaked
1 cup shredded Swiss cheese
½ cup freshly grated Parmesan cheese
1 tablespoon unsalted butter
8 ounces fresh button mushrooms, sliced

3 eggs
1 cup heavy whipping cream
dash of white pepper
¼ teaspoon coarse salt
1½ teaspoons Worcestershire sauce

Preheat the oven to 350°F. Place the pie crust in a 9-inch pie pan; sprinkle with the Swiss and Parmesan cheeses. In a sauté pan, melt the butter over medium heat. Sauté the mushrooms until softened, about 5 minutes. Pour the mushrooms into the pie shell. In a medium bowl, beat together the eggs, cream, white pepper, salt and Worcestershire, and pour the mixture over the cheese and mushrooms. Bake until golden and set, about 35 minutes. Cool slightly before cutting and serve warm.

HERBED TOMATO BRIE PIE

SERVES 6 *to* 8

Refined yet casual, this Brie pie is perfectly paired with a fresh green salad and crusty French bread.
The recipe calls for you to "parbake" the crust, which means to bake it partially.

1 refrigerated pie crust, unbaked
4 vine-ripened tomatoes
5 ounces Brie, rind removed and cut into small cubes
3 ounces fresh mozzarella, cut into small cubes
coarse salt and freshly ground pepper

¼ cup fresh basil chiffonade
2 tablespoons snipped fresh chives
3 eggs
⅓ cup heavy whipping cream
⅓ cup milk

Preheat the oven to 350°F. Place the pie crust into a 9-inch pie pan. Parbake the crust for 5 to 7 minutes and remove from the oven; leave the oven on. While the crust is baking, cut each tomato into 8 wedges and remove the core and seeds. Thoroughly drain the tomatoes on paper towels. Scatter the cheese cubes onto the prepared crust. Place the tomato wedges in a spiral pattern over the cheese to cover. Season with salt and pepper, and top with the basil and chives. In a small bowl, beat the eggs, cream and milk together. Pour over the tomatoes. Bake the pie for 45 minutes or until the center is set. Allow to cool slightly before serving.

STUFFED RED PEPPERS *with* CHEESY POLENTA *and* BLACK BEANS

SERVES 6 *to* 8

This striking dish blends many favorite Mexican flavors in one colorful combination.

6 small red bell peppers, tops removed,
  seeds and membranes discarded
¾ cup dry polenta
3 cloves garlic, minced
¾ teaspoon coarse salt
¼ teaspoon freshly ground pepper
½ cup half-and-half

7 ounces canned diced green chiles
⅓ cup chopped fresh cilantro, plus additional
2 cups shredded cheddar cheese
½ cup grated Mexican cotija cheese
  (or substitute grated Parmesan cheese)
15 ounces canned black beans

Preheat the oven to 450°F. Place the bell pepper cups in a lightly oiled 9 by 13-inch baking dish. Whisk together the polenta, garlic, 2 cups of water, salt and pepper in a large saucepan over medium heat. Cook, whisking constantly, for 5 to 7 minutes or until the polenta thickens and is creamy. Stir in the half-and-half, chiles, cilantro and cheeses, blending well. Divide the black beans among the pepper cups and top with polenta. Bake for 25 to 30 minutes or until the peppers are tender. Garnish with cilantro.

Spinach and Mushroom Enchiladas with Cilantro Cream Sauce, PAGE 97

SPINACH *and* MUSHROOM ENCHILADAS *with* CILANTRO CREAM SAUCE

SERVES 4 *to* 6

The Cilantro Cream Sauce makes this enchilada dish a little decadent.
For a special presentation, line the center of the tortillas with fresh spinach leaves before filling and rolling them.

Cilantro Cream Sauce:
3 cups heavy whipping cream
¼ teaspoon cayenne pepper
1½ teaspoons coarse salt
3 cups chopped cilantro leaves (about 1 bunch)
5 teaspoons cornstarch dissolved in 5 teaspoons cold water

Enchiladas:
1 teaspoon butter
½ large onion, diced
8 ounces fresh button mushrooms, stemmed and quartered

20 ounces frozen chopped spinach, cooked
½ cup stale bread crumbs
1 teaspoon white pepper
⅛ teaspoon nutmeg
¼ teaspoon chili powder
1 egg
coarse salt
2 cups shredded Mexican blend cheese, divided
10 flour tortillas

Mix together the cream, cayenne, salt, cilantro and the dissolved cornstarch in a 2-quart saucepan over medium heat. Cook and stir until thickened, about 10 to 15 minutes. Preheat the oven to 350°F. Melt the butter in a skillet over medium heat. Add the onions and mushrooms, and sauté until the onions are transparent. Remove from heat and set aside. Squeeze the excess water out of the cooked spinach. Place the spinach, bread crumbs, white pepper, nutmeg, chili powder and egg in a food processor and pulse until blended thoroughly; season with salt. Transfer the spinach mixture to a large mixing bowl and stir in the reserved onion-mushroom mixture and 1 cup of the cheese. Spoon about ¼ cup of the filling onto each flour tortilla, roll up and place seam side down in a 9 by 13-inch baking dish. Pour the *Cilantro Cream Sauce* evenly over the enchiladas and sprinkle with the remaining 1 cup of cheese. Bake for 30 minutes or until brown and bubbly.

BLACK BEAN *and* MANGO ENCHILADAS

SERVES 4 *to* 6

The unusual combination of ingredients gives these enchiladas a tangy and tropical flair.
If mangoes are not available, substitute fresh pineapple or peaches.

1½ cups shredded cheddar cheese, divided
1½ cups shredded Monterey Jack cheese, divided
2 teaspoons vegetable oil
1 medium yellow onion, chopped
1 medium red bell pepper, seeded and chopped
3½ cups pitted, peeled and chopped fresh mangoes
   (about 2 large)
22 ounces canned black beans, drained and rinsed

¼ cup minced pickled jalapeños
3 tablespoons fresh lime juice, divided
1 teaspoon salt
½ cup chopped fresh cilantro
15 to 20 ounces canned mild red enchilada sauce
10 whole wheat flour tortillas
½ cup sour cream
1 avocado, pitted, peeled and sliced

Preheat the oven to 350°F. Lightly coat a 9 by 13-inch baking dish with cooking spray. Mix together the two cheeses in a small bowl and set aside. Heat the oil in a skillet over medium. Add the onions and bell pepper, and sauté for 5 minutes or until softened. Add the mangoes, beans, jalapeños, 1 tablespoon of the lime juice and the salt; cook until the mixture is thoroughly heated. Remove from heat. Stir in the cilantro and 2 cups of the reserved cheese. Spread 1 tablespoon of the enchilada sauce onto each tortilla. Spoon approximately ½ cup of the mango-bean mixture onto each tortilla. Roll up the tortillas and place seam side down in the baking dish.

Mix the remaining 2 tablespoons of lime juice with the remaining enchilada sauce in a bowl. Pour the mixture over the enchiladas and top with the remaining 1 cup of cheese. Spray a sheet of foil with cooking spray and wrap tightly, sprayed side down, over the dish. Bake for 30 minutes. Remove the foil and bake an additional 8 to 10 minutes or until the cheese is melted and the sauce is bubbly. Top each serving with a dollop of sour cream and an avocado slice.

from the

garden

menu sampler

THE PICNIC BASKET

Tuna Pan Bagnat

Tomato Basil Couscous Salad

*Summer Watermelon Salad with
Honey Orange Vinaigrette*

La Ciambella with Strawberries Eric

Blackberry Shortbread Bars

Lavender Lemonade

☙

A MIDSUMMER NIGHT'S DINNER

White Gazpacho

*Seared Yellowfin Tuna Salad with
Wasabi Vinaigrette*

Fresh Ciabatta Bread

Meyer Lemon Pistachio Tart

Selection of Sliced Melons

Selection of Cold Beers

☙

GARDEN PARTY

Tea Sandwiches

*Prosciutto and Orange Salad with
Honey Balsamic Vinaigrette*

Spiced Layer Cake with Berry Filling

*Shortbread Cookies with
Perfect Icing*

Lemon Coconut Cookies

Melon Slush

garden party

Spiced Layer Cake with Berry Filling, PAGE 241

Roasted Red Pepper and Three Cheese Spread, PAGE 91
and Cranberry Tarragon Chicken Salad, PAGE 118

garden party

When spring turns the garden
brilliant with color and fragrance,
outdoors is the only place to be.
Tables come out, along with crystal
cake stands, and vases and buckets
and pots overflowing with flowers.
A variety of pretty tea sandwiches,
salads and sweets are reflections
of the natural beauty that seems
to be blooming everywhere. In the
springtime air, old friendships are
refreshed and new ones are planted.

garden party

DETAILS

Invitations
A silver frame displays party
details on a floral notecard, keepsake
photos to be slipped in later.

Favors
A pretty assortment of
heirloom seed packets wrapped up as
a take-home reminder of friendships
that bloom and endure.

Décor
Mix old and new, and
creatively repurpose containers
(a silver champagne bucket brimming
with tulips; a garden trog filled with
linen-wrapped silverware) to update
traditional garden party décor.

Melon Slush, PAGE 118

garden party

TIPS

Stack plates at the beginning
of the buffet, silverware wrapped in
linen napkins at the end.

Do not be afraid to mix patterns
of plates, or keep it clean and
classic with all white.

Create easy flow by setting serving
tables away from the wall, allowing
guests to serve from both sides.

A drink station away from
the buffet alleviates congestion.

Arrange a pretty assortment of
individual desserts at guest tables
to be shared by all.

Shortbread Cookies with Perfect Icing, PAGE 227

Prosciutto and Orange Salad with Honey Balsamic Vinaigrette, PAGE 109

PROSCIUTTO and ORANGE SALAD with HONEY BALSAMIC VINAIGRETTE

SERVES 4

Prosciutto adds a salty bite to this picture perfect salad.

Honey Balsamic Vinaigrette:
½ cup olive oil
¼ cup white Balsamic vinegar
1 tablespoon honey
½ teaspoon coarse salt
¼ teaspoon freshly ground pepper

Whisk together the vinaigrette ingredients in a small bowl. Place the mixed greens in a large bowl. Add the avocados, oranges, prosciutto and walnuts, and toss with desired amount of the *Honey Balsamic Vinaigrette*. Serve immediately.

Salad:
5 ounces mixed baby greens
2 medium avocados, pitted, peeled and sliced
2 medium navel oranges, peeled and sectioned
¼ pound prosciutto, torn into bite-size pieces
⅓ cup chopped walnuts, toasted

✑ TOASTING NUTS ✐

To toast walnuts, pecans or cashews, arrange them in a single layer on a cookie sheet and bake at 350°F for 3 to 5 minutes, being careful not to burn them. It is easier to toast smaller nuts like pine nuts in a nonstick skillet over medium heat, turning them constantly to prevent over browning.

ORGANIC HERB SALAD with SIMPLE LEMON VINAIGRETTE

COURTESY of EXECUTIVE CHEF/OWNER MONICA POPE, T'AFIA

MAKES 4 to 6 SALADS

The herbs in this salad can be found at grocery stores, farmers markets or garden centers.
And it is well worth the effort to find them all—their combination makes this salad unforgettable.
This recipe yields plenty of dressing; store the extra in the refrigerator to use on any salad.

Simple Lemon Vinaigrette:
Makes 2¼ cups

⅛ cup lemon juice
2 cups olive oil (not extra virgin)
2 teaspoons sugar
2 teaspoons kosher salt
1 teaspoon white pepper, ground finely

Salad:
approximately ¼ cup of each of the following
   organically grown herbs:
      Italian flat leaf parsley leaves
      basil leaves, torn
      chives, snipped to ¾-inch long
      chervil leaves
      cilantro leaves
      dill sprigs
      tarragon leaves
      salad burnet leaves
      lemon balm
1 head butter lettuce, separated into cups
organically grown edible flowers (pansies, borage,
   chive blossoms, nasturtiums or calendulas)

Whisk together all the vinaigrette ingredients in a medium bowl; set aside. Pick and clean the herbs (leaves should be whole except for large basil leaves, which can be torn in half). Dress the herbs and butter lettuce lightly with the *Simple Lemon Vinaigrette*. Place the butter lettuce leaves on each plate so that they form a cup. Fill the lettuce cup with the herbs. Pick the petals off of the flowers and sprinkle over the herbs.

RADICCHIO SALAD *with* BLUE CHEESE *and* PEPPERED ALMONDS

SERVES 6

Radicchio's pleasantly bitter taste complements the almonds and blue cheese in this salad.
Radicchio leaves also make lovely, inventive cups for individual salad servings.

Peppered Almonds:
1 cup unsalted almonds, chopped or whole
2 teaspoons vegetable oil
1 teaspoon coarse salt
1½ teaspoons freshly ground black pepper
1½ teaspoons sugar

Salad:
1 head radicchio, torn
1 head butter lettuce, torn
8 ounces blue cheese, crumbled
¼ cup red wine vinegar
5 tablespoons almond oil (or olive oil)

Preheat the oven to 400°F. Place the almonds, oil, salt, pepper and sugar in a small bowl, and toss to coat. Arrange the almonds in a single layer on a baking pan. Bake for about 4 to 5 minutes until the coating is crisp and the almonds are toasted, stirring occasionally; set aside to cool. In a large serving bowl, combine the lettuces and blue cheese. Combine the vinegar and almond oil and drizzle over the salad. Sprinkle with the almonds and toss gently.

> ### ✂ BUTTER LETTUCE ✄
>
> *Butter lettuce is a loose head lettuce. Among its varieties are red, green and the more common Boston bibb. Butter lettuces have soft leaves and add a subtly sweet flavor to any salad.*

BEET *and* BLOOD ORANGE SALAD

SERVES 8

This beautiful salad brings vibrant color and a rich earthy flavor to a holiday table.
Be careful when preparing beets—they stain fingers and countertops. Wear latex gloves and work on a protected surface.

3 medium golden beets
2 medium red beets
3 to 4 tablespoons extra virgin olive oil, divided
3 blood oranges
1 bulb baby fennel, sliced very thin
2 tablespoons chopped fresh Italian flat leaf parsley

1 small shallot, sliced into thin rings
¼ cup unsalted roasted pistachios
1 tablespoon white Balsamic vinegar
coarse salt and freshly ground pepper
1 head butter lettuce, torn
4 ounces goat or feta cheese, crumbled

> ### ✂ BLOOD ORANGES ✄
>
> *Although blood oranges may look like typical oranges on the outside, inside they are dark red. They are sweeter and less acidic than other oranges and are in season mainly during the winter months. Blood oranges are good in salads and desserts, and give a burst of color when used as a garnish.*

Preheat the oven to 450°F. Wash the beets and cut off the ends. Rub the beets generously with 1 to 2 tablespoons of the olive oil and wrap loosely in foil, crimping to close. Roast until tender, about 1½ hours. Remove from the oven, open the foil and let cool. Peel and cut each beet into 8 wedges; set aside in a large bowl. Over a small bowl catching the juice, cut the peel and pith off the oranges and remove the sections by cutting between the membranes with a sharp knife. Add the orange sections to the beets, then add the fennel, parsley, shallots and pistachios. Whisk the vinegar and 2 tablespoons of the olive oil into the reserved orange juice; season with salt and pepper. Add the dressing to the beet-blood orange mixture and toss gently. Place the lettuce on individual salad plates; top with equal amounts of the beet-blood orange mixture and sprinkle with the cheese. Serve immediately.

110

Radicchio Salad with Blue Cheese and Peppered Almonds, PAGE 110

Fresh Tomato Salad with Herbed Dressing, PAGE 113

VIETNAMESE PORK TENDERLOIN *and* RICE NOODLE SALAD

SERVES 4 *to* 6

Use thin rice vermicelli noodles rather than regular rice noodles (which are slightly thicker and can become gummy after they are cooked).
Substitute 3 tablespoons of soy sauce and 1 teaspoon of anchovy paste if you cannot find fish sauce.

Vinaigrette:
2 cloves garlic, minced
½ teaspoon ground chili paste or Asian chili pepper sauce
3 tablespoons sugar
½ cup hot water
3 tablespoons bottled fish sauce
1½ tablespoons fresh lime juice
2 tablespoons rice wine vinegar
½ teaspoon coarse salt

Pork:
1 tablespoon brown sugar
¼ teaspoon cayenne pepper
¼ teaspoon garlic powder

½ teaspoon coarse salt
freshly ground pepper
1 pound pork tenderloin, trimmed

Salad:
8 ounces thin rice vermicelli
1 English cucumber, cut into matchsticks
2 carrots, peeled and cut into matchsticks
1 cup fresh bean sprouts
2 cups red leaf lettuce, torn
2 tablespoons each chopped mint, cilantro and basil,
    for garnish (use Thai basil if available)
3 tablespoons chopped peanuts, for garnish

Purée the garlic, chili paste, sugar and water in a small food processor. Transfer the mixture to a small saucepan. Add the fish sauce, lime juice, vinegar and salt, stirring over medium heat until the sugar dissolves, about 2 minutes. Let cool.

Combine the brown sugar, cayenne, garlic powder, salt and pepper in a small bowl and stir with a fork. On a large piece of foil, sprinkle the spice rub over the pork tenderloin, cover tightly with the foil and seal; chill for at least 30 minutes or as long as overnight. Preheat the oven to 375°F. Remove the foil and place the tenderloin on a lightly oiled roasting pan. Roast for 30 minutes or until a meat thermometer inserted in the center reads 145°F. When done, place the tenderloin on a cutting board and allow it to rest for about 15 minutes or until the internal temperature reaches 160°F. Cut into ½-inch slices and then cut into ¼-inch strips.

Bring a pot of water to a boil and add the vermicelli. Boil the noodles for about 3 minutes until soft or according to package directions. Drain and rinse under cold water and set aside to cool. If the noodles start to stick together as they cool, toss them in a bowl with a small amount of the vinaigrette. In a large bowl, toss together the cucumber, carrots, bean sprouts, noodles and desired amount of the vinaigrette. In a large serving bowl, layer the lettuce, noodle mixture and pork. Garnish with the chopped herbs and peanuts. Serve at room temperature.

STEAK, PEAR *and* WALNUT SALAD

SERVES 4 *to* 6

The classic steakhouse flavors of beef and blue cheese are captured in this impressive salad.

1 pound New York strip steaks
1 clove garlic, minced
coarse salt and freshly ground pepper
2 ripe but firm Bartlett pears, cut into ¼-inch slices
1 head Romaine lettuce, stems and ribs removed, torn

5 ounces field greens
4 ounces crumbled blue cheese
⅓ cup walnut pieces, toasted
olive oil
Balsamic vinegar

Coat the grill with cooking spray and preheat on high. Cover the steaks with the garlic and season with salt and pepper. Reduce the grill to medium heat and cook the steaks and pear slices for 3 to 5 minutes per side. Remove the pears when browned but still crisp; cut into strips. Remove the steaks when they reach desired doneness. Trim the excess fat from the steaks and cut into thin slices. Toss the greens with the steak, pears, blue cheese and walnuts; drizzle with olive oil and vinegar, and serve immediately.

CHOPPED CHICKEN SALAD *with* CHIPOTLE LIME VINAIGRETTE

SERVES 6 *to* 8

The heart of this salad is its intensely flavored vinaigrette.
Toss in other Mexican favorites (jicama, black beans, avocado) for different textures and tastes.

Chipotle Lime Vinaigrette:
⅓ cup rice wine vinegar
¼ cup fresh lime juice
1 clove garlic, minced
2 tablespoons honey
1 large chipotle chile in adobo sauce (about 2 teaspoons)
½ teaspoon coarse salt
¾ cup canola oil
1 cup chopped fresh cilantro

Salad:
3 ears of corn, shucked
1¼ pounds chicken breasts, cooked and cut into thin strips
1½ cups diced vine-ripened tomatoes
5 ounces mixed baby greens
2 cups shredded Monterey Jack cheese
½ cup diced roasted red bell pepper
cilantro sprigs, for garnish
¾ cup toasted hulled pumpkin seeds (pepitas), for garnish

Combine the vinegar, lime juice, garlic, honey, chile (with a little of the sauce) and salt in a food processor and blend until smooth. With the machine running, slowly add the oil in a thin stream to form an emulsion. Add the cilantro and pulse to combine.

Cut the kernels from the corn cobs with a serrated knife. Place the corn, chicken, tomatoes, greens, cheese and peppers in a large salad bowl. Toss with desired amount of the *Chipotle Lime Vinaigrette*. Before serving, garnish with the cilantro and pumpkin seeds.

GRILLED SCALLOPS *and* SHRIMP *with* SUMMER FRUIT SALAD

COURTESY *of* ELOUISE "OUISIE" ADAMS JONES, OUISIE'S TABLE

SERVES 4 *to* 6

From the Gulf Coast to the Hill Country to the Piney Woods, this summer salad is a culinary tour of Texas.

Ginger Vinaigrette:
½ cup extra virgin olive oil
2 tablespoons peeled and minced fresh ginger
2 tablespoons fresh lime juice
1 tablespoon sherry vinegar
coarse salt and freshly ground pepper

Salad:
8 fresh or frozen jumbo shrimp in shells (about 8 ounces)
8 large sea scallops (about 12 ounces)
2 tablespoons extra virgin olive oil

1 tablespoon snipped fresh Italian flat leaf parsley
2 teaspoons snipped fresh rosemary
1 teaspoon snipped fresh thyme
½ teaspoon kosher salt
¼ teaspoon freshly ground black pepper
8 ounces mesclun greens (12 cups)
4 ripe Texas Hill Country peaches or small ripe peaches, halved, pitted and sliced (peeling optional)
1 medium mango, peeled, pitted and sliced
1 cup fresh blueberries
½ cup fresh mint leaves

Whisk together the olive oil, ginger, lime juice and vinegar in a small bowl, and season with salt and pepper; set aside. Thaw the shrimp, if frozen. Peel and devein, leaving the tails intact. Rinse the shrimp; pat dry. In a large bowl gently toss together the shrimp, scallops, olive oil, parsley, rosemary, thyme, salt and pepper. Thread the shrimp and scallops onto 4 long metal skewers. For a charcoal grill, grill the kabobs on the greased rack of an uncovered grill directly over medium coals. Cook for 10 minutes or until the shrimp and scallops are opaque, turning once. (For a gas grill, preheat the grill. Reduce heat to medium. Place the kabobs on a greased grill rack over heat. Cover and grill as above.)

Meanwhile, in a very large bowl combine the mesclun, peaches, mango, blueberries and mint. Drizzle three-fourths of the *Ginger Vinaigrette* over the greens mixture, tossing gently to coat. Transfer the greens mixture to a large serving platter. Top with the grilled shrimp and scallops. Drizzle the desired amount of the remaining vinaigrette over the salad. Serve with any remaining vinaigrette.

Chopped Chicken Salad with Chipotle Lime Vinaigrette, PAGE 124

Tuna Niçoise Salad, PAGE 127

TUNA NIÇOISE SALAD

This interpretation of the French classic integrates farm fresh ingredients and a bright citrus dressing.

Dressing:
6 tablespoons extra virgin olive oil
2 tablespoons fresh lemon juice
2 tablespoons freshly squeezed orange juice
2 to 3 teaspoons Dijon mustard
coarse salt

Salad:
1 pound baby new potatoes, boiled and cooled
coarse salt and freshly ground pepper

2 heads butter or other leafy lettuce
4 eggs, hard-boiled and cut in half lengthwise
½ pound haricot verts or thin green beans,
    blanched and chilled
1 red or yellow bell pepper, seeded and thinly sliced
1 pint cherry or grape tomatoes
½ English cucumber, thinly sliced
1 small fennel bulb, thinly sliced
13 ounces premium white meat tuna, drained
¾ cup Kalamata olives

Whisk together the dressing ingredients in a small bowl; season with salt. Cut the potatoes in half and coat lightly with about half of the dressing. Season with salt and pepper and set aside. Place large pieces of lettuce on the bottom of a serving platter. Starting with the potatoes on one side, arrange the remaining ingredients in groups on the platter. Drizzle with the remaining dressing and serve.

SEARED YELLOWFIN TUNA SALAD *with* WASABI VINAIGRETTE

This salad satisfies cravings for the distinctive pairing of tuna and wasabi.
Since the fish is served rare, purchase sashimi grade only and serve it the same day you buy it.

Wasabi Vinaigrette:
1 teaspoon wasabi paste
1½ tablespoons rice wine vinegar
1½ tablespoons soy sauce
5 tablespoons extra virgin olive oil
coarse salt and freshly ground pepper

Tuna:
2 tablespoons dark sesame oil
2 tablespoons soy sauce
1 tablespoon peeled and grated fresh ginger

1 clove garlic, minced
1 teaspoon fresh lime juice
2 sashimi grade yellowfin tuna steaks, 6 to 8 ounces each
sesame seeds
freshly ground pepper

Salad:
5 ounces mixed baby greens
4 radishes, sliced
½ cup sliced English cucumber
green onion curls, for garnish

Whisk together the vinaigrette ingredients in a medium bowl until well combined; season with salt and pepper, and set aside.

Mix together the sesame oil, soy sauce, ginger, garlic and lime juice in a small bowl. Place the tuna steaks in a small baking dish, cover with the marinade, wrap tightly and refrigerate for at least 1 hour. Heat a skillet over medium-high. Remove the tuna from the marinade, and coat generously with sesame seeds and pepper. Sear the tuna for 1 to 1½ minutes on all sides (or longer for tuna that is cooked through). Remove the tuna and cut into ¼-inch slices.

Combine the greens, radishes and cucumbers in a large bowl. Divide the salad between 2 plates and top with the tuna slices. Drizzle the salad with the vinaigrette and garnish with green onions. Serve immediately.

pizzas ar

d pastas

menu sampler

THE FAMILY TABLE

Spinach Tortellini Casserole

Roasted Cherry Tomatoes

Selection of Grilled Sausage

Cookies and Cream Bites

CROWD PLEASER

Bruschetta and Crostini Sampler

*Radicchio Salad with Blue Cheese
and Peppered Almonds*

Farmers Market Lasagna

Homestyle Spaghetti with Meat Sauce

Chocolate Chip Biscotti

Selection of Italian Gelati

AL FRESCO GATHERING

Caipirinha Cocktail

*Fresh Tomato Salad
with Herbed Dressing*

*Grilled Tuscan Shrimp
with Lemon Orzo*

Grilled Pizza

Grilled Marinated Vegetables

*Almond Apricot Cake
with Crème Fraîche*

Grilled Pizza, PAGE 132

GRILLED PIZZA *with* PEAR, ARUGULA *and* TRUFFLE OIL

MAKES 4 *to* 6 INDIVIDUAL PIZZAS

Grilling gives pizza a distinctively crisp crust and smoky flavor.
Grilled pizza bread without toppings is also delicious served with an olive oil and herb dipping sauce.
Pizza dough can be made ahead and frozen to use later.

Crust:
1½ cups warm water
2 (.25 ounce) envelopes active dry yeast
  or 2 scant tablespoons
1 tablespoon sugar
3 tablespoons olive oil
3½ cups all-purpose flour, divided, plus extra
½ cup whole wheat flour
1 tablespoon coarse salt
cornmeal

Topping:
2 cups fresh arugula
garlic-infused olive oil
3 ounces chèvre, softened
½ pear, cored and sliced
truffle oil

Crust: Lightly oil a large bowl and set aside. Combine the water, yeast, sugar and olive oil in a large bowl; carefully whisk to combine. Let stand for several minutes until the yeast dissolves. Add both types of flour and the salt, and mix well. This can be done with a stand mixer or by hand. Knead the dough on a lightly floured surface until smooth, about 3 to 5 minutes, sprinkling with additional flour as needed. When the dough is ready, place in the oiled bowl and turn to coat; cover with a towel or plastic wrap and set aside in a warm place. Let rise until about double in size, about 30 minutes. Punch down and divide the dough into 4 to 6 equal parts, roll into balls and place on a baking sheet. Cover with a warm damp towel, return to a warm place and allow the dough to rest for at least 15 minutes. On a lightly floured surface, roll and stretch each ball into an 8 to 10-inch circle and place on a baking sheet covered with cornmeal. Lightly oil the grill and heat to medium-high.

Topping: Drizzle the arugula with the olive oil and toss gently to combine; chill. Place the dough on the grill and cook for 1 to 2 minutes or until slightly puffed. Flip and cook until the crust is crisp, about 5 more minutes. Spread the chèvre on the crust and place the pears in a circle. Cook just until warmed. Remove from the grill. Top with the arugula and drizzle with a few drops of the truffle oil.

Alternative toppings: Instead of pears and arugula, try topping the pizza crust with one of these combinations:

Rustic Chicken Pesto Pizza:
½ cup prepared basil pesto
1 cup cooked shredded chicken
½ cup roasted red bell peppers
2 cups shredded mozzarella cheese

Margherita Pizza:
garlic-infused olive oil
8 ounces fresh mozzarella cheese, sliced
2 to 3 fresh Roma tomatoes, sliced
½ cup fresh basil chiffonade

✎ GRILLED MARINATED VEGETABLES ✎

6 to 8 cups thickly sliced vegetables

Vinaigrette:
⅔ cup Balsamic vinegar
2 tablespoons Dijon mustard
3 tablespoons olive oil
¼ teaspoon salt
¼ teaspoon pepper
4 cloves garlic, minced

Combine your favorite sliced vegetables such as yellow squash, zucchini, green onions, eggplant, asparagus, and yellow, red and orange bell peppers in a gallon-size resealable plastic bag. Combine the vinaigrette ingredients and pour into the bag of vegetables. Seal and marinate for 30 minutes. Remove the vegetables from the bag and place in a wire grilling basket coated with cooking spray, or on a cookie sheet if using a broiler. Grill or broil the vegetables for 5 to 7 minutes on each side or until tender.

DEEP DISH SPINACH PIZZA

SERVES 4 to 6

*This delicious pizza takes time and is worth the effort. To simplify meal preparation, make the dough ahead of time
(or use prepared dough from your grocery store or favorite pizzeria), and use prepared pizza sauce. For a thin crust version,
roll out the dough to desired thickness and bake on a cornmeal-dusted pizza stone or baking sheet.*

Crust:
1 cup warm water
.25 ounce envelope active dry yeast (1 scant tablespoon)
pinch of sugar
2 to 2¼ cups all-purpose flour
1 cup whole wheat flour
1 teaspoon salt
2 tablespoons olive oil
cornmeal

Sauce:
2 tablespoons olive oil
1 medium onion, sliced
2 teaspoons finely minced garlic
16 ounces canned diced tomatoes, undrained
¼ teaspoon salt
¼ teaspoon sugar
pinch of crushed red pepper

Topping:
2 tablespoons olive oil
6 cloves garlic, finely minced, or less to taste
1½ pounds fresh baby spinach, washed but not dried
2 teaspoons coarse salt
2 cups shredded Italian blend cheese
    (mozzarella, Parmesan, Asiago), divided
16 fresh basil leaves
2 to 3 ripe plum or small round tomatoes,
sliced thinly into rounds
1 small green bell pepper,
    seeded and sliced into ¼-inch strips
1 small red bell pepper,
    seeded and sliced into ¼-inch strips

133

Crust: Lightly oil a large bowl and set aside. Place the water in a small bowl; add the yeast and sugar, stirring until dissolved. Let the mixture stand in a warm place until bubbly. In a food processor (or by hand or using a mixer fitted with a dough paddle), mix together 2 cups of the all-purpose flour, the whole wheat flour and salt; blend. Add the olive oil to the yeast mixture and gradually mix it into the flour mixture until the dough is formed and pulls away from the sides of the bowl. Transfer the dough to a floured surface and knead until smooth and elastic, using up to ¼ cup more flour, a little at a time, if needed to keep the dough from sticking. Place the dough in the oiled bowl, turning to coat; cover the bowl with plastic wrap and place in a warm, draft-free place. Let the dough rise until doubled in size, about 20 minutes. Punch the dough down, cover and refrigerate until needed. Lightly grease a 9½-inch round springform pan and lightly sprinkle the bottom of the pan with cornmeal and set aside.

Sauce: Heat the olive oil in a large skillet over medium-low. Sauté the onions and garlic until soft but not brown. Reduce heat to low. Add the tomatoes, breaking up slightly; then add the salt, sugar and red pepper. Simmer the sauce, uncovered, stirring occasionally until it is very thick, about 25 to 30 minutes.

Topping: In a large pot or Dutch oven, heat the olive oil over medium and sauté the garlic for about 1 minute until soft but not brown. Add the spinach and salt to the pot and toss with the sautéed garlic and oil. Cover the pot and cook for 2 minutes. Uncover the pot, turn the heat to high and cook the spinach 1 more minute, stirring with a wooden spoon until all the spinach is wilted. Drain thoroughly and gently squeeze out any excess moisture.

Assembly: Place the oven rack on the lowest rung. Preheat the oven to 425°F. Roll out the dough on a lightly floured surface into a 12-inch circle. Line the bottom and sides of the prepared pan with the dough and trim the excess. Sprinkle 1½ cups of the cheese over the crust, then spread the tomato sauce evenly over the cheese. Next, spread the cooked spinach over the tomato sauce. Arrange some of the basil leaves in a circle along the outer edge of the pizza and top with half of the tomato slices. Use the remaining basil leaves and tomato slices to fill in the center of the pizza. Arrange the pepper slices similarly, alternating between red and green strips. Top with the remaining ½ cup of cheese. Bake the pizza for 25 minutes or until the crust is golden brown and the cheese is bubbly. Let stand for 5 minutes before removing the sides of the pan; cut and serve immediately.

SEA SCALLOPS *and* ORZO *with* CHERRY TOMATOES

SERVES 4

This pretty main course uses orzo, a rice-shaped pasta, as a base for the sweet sea scallops.
Add pine nuts and arugula for extra flavor in this colorful dish. Remember that scallops should always smell fresh, never sour.

1 cup dry orzo pasta
2 tablespoons olive oil, divided
¾ teaspoon coarse salt, divided
¼ teaspoon freshly ground pepper, divided
1 pound sea scallops
1 cup chopped sweet onion, such as Vidalia or Texas 1015

4 cloves garlic, minced
¼ teaspoon crushed red pepper
2 cups cherry, grape or cherub tomatoes, halved
⅔ cup freshly grated Pecorino Romano cheese
⅓ cup fresh basil chiffonade

Cook the orzo according to package directions. While the pasta cooks, heat 1 tablespoon of the olive oil in a large skillet over medium-high. Sprinkle ½ teaspoon of the salt and ⅛ teaspoon of the pepper evenly over the scallops. Add the scallops to the skillet and sauté for 3 minutes on each side or until done. Remove the scallops from the pan and set aside. Drain the excess liquid from the pan and add the remaining 1 tablespoon of olive oil. Add the onions, garlic and red pepper, and cook for 2 minutes, stirring frequently. Stir in the pasta and scallops, and continue to cook for 1 minute or until heated through. Remove from heat, season with the remaining salt and pepper, and stir in the tomatoes, cheese and basil.

ORZO *with* ITALIAN SAUSAGE *and* WILD MUSHROOMS

SERVES 8

Madeira wine, which is fortified with brandy, comes from a small volcanic island off the coast of Portugal.
It is often used for cooking rather than sipping, but can also be enjoyed as an apéritif or dessert wine. It infuses the orzo in this dish
with a rich, sweet flavor. If you do not have Madeira wine on hand, dry port or sherry is a good substitute.

8 ounces portobello mushrooms, stemmed
2 tablespoons olive oil
1 pound sweet Italian sausage, casings removed
10 ounces fresh shiitake mushrooms, stemmed and diced
1 teaspoon chopped fresh thyme
1 teaspoon chopped fresh oregano
1½ cups Madeira wine or sherry, divided
4 cups chicken broth

4 tablespoons (½ stick) butter
1 large onion, chopped
4 cloves garlic, minced
16 ounces orzo pasta
3 cups heavy whipping cream, divided
coarse salt and freshly ground pepper
1 cup freshly grated Asiago cheese

Prepare the portobello mushrooms by scraping out the gills and dicing. Heat the olive oil in a large skillet over medium-high. Add the sausage and sauté until it begins to brown, about 3 minutes; use a spoon to break up the meat. Add the mushrooms, thyme and oregano, and sauté until the mushrooms are tender, about 20 minutes. Add ½ cup of the Madeira and boil until it is almost absorbed, about 1 minute; set aside. Bring the broth to a simmer in a large saucepan; remove from heat and cover to keep warm. In a heavy stockpot, melt the butter over medium-high heat. Add the onions and garlic; sauté until the onion is translucent, about 5 minutes. Add the orzo and stir for 2 minutes. Add the remaining 1 cup of Madeira and simmer until absorbed, about 2 minutes. Add 1 cup of the hot broth and 1 cup of the cream, and simmer until almost absorbed, stirring often, about 3 minutes. Continue to add more broth and cream 1 cup at a time. Stirring continuously, allow most of the liquid to be absorbed before adding more. Stir and simmer about 25 minutes, or until the pasta is just tender and the mixture is creamy. Stir in the sausage mixture and season with salt and pepper. Transfer the orzo to a serving bowl and top with the cheese.

Sea Scallops and Orzo with Cherry Tomatoes, PAGE 134

"Out of the Box" Macaroni and Cheese, PAGE 137

"OUT *of the* BOX" MACARONI *and* CHEESE
SERVES 4 *to* 6

Short, hollow pastas like cavatappi or rigatoni go well with thick sauces, in part because they trap the sauce.
They are also good for baked dishes because they have considerable body and can withstand being heated a second time.
Play with the cheeses in this recipe—try aged cheddar, goat cheese or Emmenthaler in the mix.
To make this grownup macaroni and cheese an entrée, add prosciutto and peas.

5½ tablespoons butter, divided
¾ cup panko bread crumbs
¼ cup freshly grated Parmigiano-Reggiano cheese
¼ cup plus 2 tablespoons all-purpose flour
3 cups whole milk

1 teaspoon coarse salt
⅛ teaspoon freshly ground black pepper
8 ounces finely shredded Gruyére cheese
¾ cup mascarpone cheese
½ pound (8 ounces) cavatappi or other hollow pasta

Preheat the oven to 350°F. Bring a large pot of water to a boil. Meanwhile, in a small saucepan, melt 2½ tablespoons of the butter over low heat. Add the panko and Parmigiano-Reggiano cheese, toss well and set aside. Melt the remaining 3 tablespoons of butter in a large saucepan over low heat. Add the flour and stir frequently for 5 minutes, not letting the flour brown. Gradually whisk in the milk and cook for 5 minutes, whisking constantly. Add the salt, pepper, Gruyére and mascarpone, and continue to whisk until the cheese melts; remove from heat (mixture may be thin). Add the pasta to the boiling water and cook until al dente, about 8 minutes. Drain the pasta and return to the pot; pour the cheese sauce over the pasta and mix well. Pour the pasta mixture into a 9 by 13-inch baking dish and sprinkle with the panko mixture. Bake until golden brown and bubbly, about 30 to 45 minutes.

HOMESTYLE SPAGHETTI *with* MEAT SAUCE
SERVES 4 *to* 6

A homestyle sauce is easier to make than you might think and tastes much better than prepared varieties.
For a thinner sauce, purée the canned tomatoes in a blender or food processor and add ½ cup water.
For a thicker sauce, add 2 to 3 additional tablespoons of tomato paste.

2 tablespoons olive oil
1 carrot, peeled and diced to ¼-inch
1 stalk celery, diced to ¼-inch
½ yellow onion, diced
¼ cup chopped fresh parsley
2 cloves garlic, minced
½ pound Italian sausage, casings removed
1 pound lean ground beef

coarse salt and freshly ground pepper
½ cup white wine
2 tablespoons tomato paste
28 ounces canned plum tomatoes, undrained
16 ounces spaghetti, cooked according to package directions
freshly grated Parmigiano-Reggiano cheese, for garnish

Heat the olive oil in a large sauté pan over medium-low. Add the diced vegetables, parsley, garlic and sausage, and cook for 15 minutes or until the vegetables are tender. Increase the heat to medium. Add the beef and brown; drain the fat only if desired. Season with salt and pepper. Add the white wine and stir, allowing the wine to evaporate. Stir in the tomato paste until combined, then add the tomatoes. Bring the sauce to a boil, then reduce heat to low and allow the sauce to simmer uncovered for 30 minutes, stirring occasionally. Combine the sauce with the cooked spaghetti and serve with the cheese.

> ∽ TOMATO PASTE ∾
>
> *Look for tomato paste in a tube (usually found near the prepared pasta sauce). Once you have used what you need, store the rest in the refrigerator rather than throw out half a can of unused paste. If you cannot find tomato paste in a tube, freeze leftover canned paste in an ice cube tray, then transfer to a plastic bag to store in the freezer.*

GNOCCHI *with* PANCETTA *and* WATERCRESS
SERVES 4
Pancetta, an Italian meat similar to bacon, adds a peppery flavor to the gnocchi and watercress. A type of pork that has been salt-cured, spiced and dried for about three months, its taste varies depending on where in Italy it was produced.

2 ounces pancetta, chopped
3 cloves garlic, minced
2 large tomatoes, chopped
½ teaspoon sugar
¼ teaspoon crushed red pepper
2 teaspoons red wine vinegar

½ teaspoon coarse salt
1 pound gnocchi (shelf-stable, fresh or frozen)
4 ounces watercress, tough stems removed,
   coarsely chopped (6 cups packed)
⅓ cup freshly grated Parmigiano-Reggiano cheese

Bring a large pot of water to a boil. Cook the pancetta in a large nonstick skillet over medium heat until it begins to brown, about 4 to 5 minutes; stir occasionally. Add the garlic and sauté for 30 seconds. Add the tomatoes, sugar and red pepper, and cook, stirring, until the tomatoes are almost completely broken down, about 5 minutes. Stir in the vinegar and salt; remove from heat. Cook the gnocchi in boiling water until they float, according to package directions. Place the watercress in a colander and drain the gnocchi over the watercress; the hot water will wilt the watercress slightly. Add the gnocchi and watercress to the sauce in the pan; toss to combine. Serve immediately topped with the cheese.

ORECCHIETTE *with* CARAMELIZED ONIONS, CHICKEN SAUSAGE *and* RICOTTA SALATA
SERVES 6
Ricotta salata is a salty Italian sheep's milk cheese, similar in flavor to Greek feta. It is available at specialty food stores and some grocery stores. If you cannot find ricotta salata, substitute 2 ounces of crumbled feta cheese.

12 ounces dried orecchiette pasta
3 tablespoons butter
1 onion, peeled and thinly sliced
2 large cloves garlic, minced
¼ teaspoon crushed red pepper

8 ounces chicken sausage,
   removed from casings and crumbled
1 pound ripe tomatoes, rinsed, cored and chopped
1 cup frozen peas, thawed
4 ounces ricotta salata cheese, thinly sliced or crumbled

In a medium pan over high heat, bring 4 quarts of water to a boil. Add the pasta and cook, stirring occasionally, until tender to the bite, 12 to 15 minutes; drain. Meanwhile, in a skillet over medium heat, melt the butter. Add the onions and stir often until lightly browned and caramelized around the edges, about 20 minutes. Add the garlic, red pepper and sausage. Stir with a wooden spoon, breaking up the sausage if necessary, until the meat is beginning to brown, 5 to 10 minutes; if the garlic begins to scorch, lower heat. Add the tomatoes and peas, and stir for about 2 minutes until heated through. In a large bowl, mix the pasta and sauce to coat; top with the ricotta salata.

PENNE *with* SWEET ITALIAN TURKEY SAUSAGE *and* ARUGULA

SERVES 4 *to* 6

Just minutes from start to finish, this simple one dish dinner is great for any weekday meal.
Use fresh baby spinach if you cannot find arugula.

12 ounces penne pasta
2 tablespoons garlic-infused olive oil
1 pound Italian turkey sausage, casings removed
1 large onion, thinly sliced
1 cup grape tomatoes

⅛ teaspoon crushed red pepper
coarse salt
2 cups baby arugula
¾ cup freshly grated Parmesan cheese
1 cup reserved pasta water

Place the pasta in a large pot of boiling water. As the pasta is cooking, heat the olive oil in a sauté pan over medium-high. Add the sausage and brown while breaking it apart until crumbly. Add the onion slices and sauté until transparent, about 5 minutes. Add the tomatoes, red pepper and a pinch of salt to the sausage and onions. Stir to break up the tomatoes slightly. When the pasta is just short of al dente, add the arugula to the sausage mixture and stir to combine. Reserve 1 cup of the pasta water before draining the pasta. Drain the pasta and add it to the pan with the sausage mixture. Raise the heat to high and stir to coat the pasta. Add the cheese and the pasta water to the pan, stirring to create a sauce. Place the pasta in a serving bowl and drizzle with additional olive oil, if desired.

RIGATONI *with* SAUSAGE *and* BEANS

SERVES 6

Rustic peasant-style food is the inspiration for this spicy pasta.
The hint of cinnamon and nutmeg adds an aromatic warmth to this dish, and makes it perfect for cool evenings.

2 tablespoons olive oil
4 cloves garlic, minced
1 large onion, chopped
⅓ cup chopped celery
½ cup chopped carrots
1 pound hot Italian sausage, casings removed
  (turkey sausage may be substituted)
1 cup dry red wine
28 ounces canned diced tomatoes, undrained

½ teaspoon cayenne pepper
pinch of cinnamon
pinch of nutmeg
coarse salt and freshly ground pepper
1 pound rigatoni pasta
19 ounces canned cannellini beans, drained
¾ cup freshly grated Parmesan cheese, divided
2 tablespoons butter
4 tablespoons fresh basil chiffonade, divided

Bring a large pot of water to a boil. In a large skillet, heat the olive oil over medium. Add the garlic and sauté until softened. Add the onions, celery, carrots and sausage. Use a spoon to break up the meat and cook until browned, about 7 minutes.

Add the wine and cook until reduced by half. Stir in the tomatoes, cayenne, cinnamon and nutmeg; season with salt and pepper. Cook over medium heat until slightly thickened. Add the pasta to the boiling water and cook according to package directions. Reserve 1 cup of the cooking water, then drain the pasta. Add the pasta to the sauce and stir gently. Add the beans, ½ cup of the cheese, the butter and 3 tablespoons of the basil. Stir gently until heated through. Add some of the reserved cooking water if the pasta looks dry. Place the pasta in a large serving bowl and garnish with the remaining ¼ cup of cheese and tablespoon of basil.

> ❧ BASIL CHIFFONADE ❧
>
> *Layer the leaves of basil on top of each other and roll them up lengthwise. Use a sharp knife or kitchen scissors to slice the basil into thin strips from top to bottom, leaving beautiful streamers of thin-cut basil. This is the best way to cut basil, because leaves do not get as bruised as they do with chopping and they keep all their color and texture.*

PARMESAN RISOTTO

SERVES 4 *to* 6

Basic Italian risotto can be served as a simple side dish or embellished with other flavors to match any menu.

3 to 4 cups low-sodium chicken broth
4 tablespoons unsalted butter, divided
1 medium onion, finely chopped
1 clove garlic, minced
1½ cups Arborio or Carnaroli rice

1 cup dry white wine
½ teaspoon coarse salt
¼ teaspoon freshly ground pepper
½ cup freshly grated Parmesan cheese, plus additional
3 tablespoons fresh Italian flat leaf parsley, chopped

In a medium saucepan, bring the broth to a simmer and keep warm over low heat. In a separate saucepan, melt 2 tablespoons of the butter over medium heat. Add the onions and garlic and cook, stirring with a wooden spoon, until the onions are transparent, about 5 minutes. Add the rice and cook, stirring, until it is well coated with the butter and starts to turn translucent, about 2 minutes. Add the wine and simmer gently, stirring, until all the liquid is absorbed, 3 to 5 minutes. Ladle ½ cup of the warm broth into the rice mixture and simmer, stirring occasionally, until the broth is absorbed. Repeat, adding ½ cup of broth at a time, until the rice is cooked through but still firm, 20 to 25 minutes total. Add the remaining 2 tablespoons of butter and the salt, pepper and Parmesan. Stir to incorporate. Adjust seasonings as desired. Serve immediately, topping with additional grated Parmesan and the parsley.

∽ RISOTTO IDEAS ∾

Other ingredients can easily be added to the basic risotto recipe (above). Simply replace the Parmesan cheese with one of the following (or some of your own favorite ingredients):

- *2 roasted red peppers, peeled, seeded and puréed in ½ cup chicken broth or water*
- *1½ cups pure pumpkin purée, topping the risotto with fried sage or toasted hazelnuts*
- *1 cup chopped poached or rotisserie chicken and 1 tablespoon fresh chopped thyme*
- *1 cup halved cherry tomatoes and ½ cup basil chiffonade*
- *1 pound asparagus, tough ends removed, blanched and chopped, plus 1 cup thawed frozen peas*

SPINACH TORTELLINI CASSEROLE

SERVES 6 *to* 8

This simple baked pasta makes a satisfying weeknight dinner, or a unique side dish with grilled meats or chicken.

2 packages (10 ounces each) fresh cheese tortellini,
  cooked according to package directions
2 tablespoons olive oil
¾ cup chopped onion
1 clove garlic, minced

10 ounces frozen spinach, thawed and drained
2 cups heavy whipping cream
2 cups freshly grated Parmigiano-Reggiano cheese, divided
coarse salt and freshly ground pepper

Preheat the oven to 350°F. Lightly butter a casserole dish; add the cooked tortellini and set aside. In a large skillet, heat the olive oil over medium and sauté the onions and garlic until soft and golden. Add the spinach, cream and 1 cup of the cheese to the pan, stirring to combine. Season with salt and pepper. Pour the spinach mixture over the tortellini and sprinkle the remaining 1 cup of cheese on top. Bake for 30 minutes.

PASTA *with* SPRING VEGETABLES IN SAFFRON CREAM SAUCE

SERVES 4

This creamy delight is best in springtime when fresh peas and asparagus abound.

1½ pounds thin asparagus
5 saffron threads
1 tablespoon butter
2 shallots, finely diced
1½ cups heavy whipping cream
½ teaspoon coarse salt

¼ teaspoon white pepper
1 pound green peas, fresh or frozen
12 ounces farfalle, orecchiette or sagnarelli pasta
¼ cup chopped fresh Italian flat leaf parsley
1 teaspoon finely grated lemon zest
freshly grated Parmigiano-Reggiano cheese

Bring a large pot of salted water to a boil. Snap off the ends of the asparagus and discard. Cut the asparagus on the diagonal into 2-inch pieces. In a small bowl, cover the saffron with 2 tablespoons of boiling water and set aside. Melt the butter in a large sauté pan over medium-low heat. Add the shallots and cook for several minutes until softened. Add the cream and the saffron with liquid. Bring to a boil, reduce heat, and add the salt and white pepper. When the pot of water has come to a boil, add the asparagus and peas. Using a slotted spoon, remove the vegetables from the water when tender but still bright green, after about 4 to 5 minutes. Gently stir the vegetables into the cream sauce; set aside. Cook the pasta in the same pot of boiling water according to package directions; drain well. Add the cooked pasta to the cream and vegetable mixture, tossing gently to coat. Add the parsley and lemon zest, and top with cheese.

GARLIC CHICKEN PASTA *with* PROSCIUTTO

SERVES 6 *to* 8

Packed with the robust flavors of garlic, roasted red peppers and basil, this pasta is reminiscent of Italy in summertime.
Fusilli and orecchiette (or other shell-shaped pastas) also work well with the ingredients in this recipe.

3 tablespoons extra virgin olive oil
1½ to 2 pounds boneless skinless chicken breasts,
   pounded thin
coarse salt and freshly ground pepper
10 to 12 cloves garlic, minced (about ¼ cup)
1 cup grape tomatoes, halved
3 ounces prosciutto, cut into small pieces
2 tablespoons butter

12 ounces farfalle pasta
½ cup fresh basil chiffonade, plus additional
½ cup prepared fire-roasted red bell peppers,
   cut into strips
½ cup freshly grated Parmigiano-Reggiano cheese,
   plus additional
¼ teaspoon crushed red pepper

Heat the olive oil in a large skillet over medium. Season the chicken with salt and pepper, and add to the skillet. Sauté until lightly browned on one side and then turn. Add the garlic and continue cooking until the garlic is soft and golden, being careful not to burn, and the chicken is cooked through, about 5 minutes. Reduce heat to medium-low, add the tomatoes, prosciutto and butter; sauté for about 5 more minutes. While the chicken is cooking, bring a large pot of water to a boil; cook the pasta according to package directions for al dente. Remove the chicken to a cutting board and cut into bite-size pieces. Return the chicken to the skillet, stir in the basil and sauté until the basil is wilted. Drain the pasta and transfer to a serving bowl. Add the chicken-tomato mixture, roasted peppers, cheese and red pepper; toss gently to combine. Top with additional basil and cheese, and serve immediately.

∽ PERFECTLY COOKED PASTA ∾

- *Use plenty of water. Note that salt adds flavor, but does not really help water boil hotter or faster. Do not add oil, it makes the pasta slippery and causes the sauce to slide right off.*

- *Stir pasta during those crucial first minutes to keep it from fusing together. Starch granules are released when pasta hits boiling water and can make it sticky.*

- *Do not rinse cooked pasta; the little bit of starch that is left at the end will add body to the sauce. Instead, immediately toss the hot pasta with sauce to let it soak up the flavor.*

Farmers Market Lasagna, PAGE 143

FARMERS MARKET LASAGNA

SERVES 6 *to* 8

Enjoy the robust flavors of this classic vegetarian taste sensation.
Eggplant, yellow squash or mushrooms may be substituted for the zucchini.

8 ounces fresh baby spinach
2 tablespoons olive oil, plus additional if needed
2 shallots, diced
¾ cup pine nuts
2 cloves garlic, minced
1 pint small cherry tomatoes, halved
2 teaspoons nutmeg
coarse salt and freshly ground pepper

8 ounces non-fat ricotta cheese
6 ounces goat cheese, room temperature
½ cup chopped fresh parsley
½ cup chopped fresh basil, plus additional
24 ounces prepared sun-dried tomato pasta sauce
9 to 12 no-boil lasagna noodles
1 large zucchini, thinly sliced into rounds
1 cup freshly grated Parmesan cheese

Preheat the oven to 350°F. Blanch the spinach in boiling water until wilted; remove to a colander and rinse with cold water. Press out the water and blot with a paper towel. Lightly oil the bottom of a 9 by 13-inch baking dish; set aside. In a large pan, heat the olive oil over medium, and sauté the shallots, pine nuts and garlic for 3 to 5 minutes, adding additional olive oil (or white wine) to keep the ingredients moist while cooking. Add the spinach, tomatoes and nutmeg. Season with salt and pepper, and continue to sauté for another 10 minutes. Remove from heat and set aside. In a bowl, stir together the ricotta and goat cheese; add the parsley and basil. To assemble the lasagna, put a very thin layer of the pasta sauce on the bottom of the prepared dish. Next, layer 3 or 4 of the lasagna noodles, half of the spinach mixture, half of the cheese mixture, half of the zucchini and top with a thin layer of sauce. Repeat the layering, beginning with another layer of lasagna noodles. Finish with a layer of lasagna noodles topped with a thin layer of sauce. Sprinkle the Parmesan cheese over the lasagna. Bake for 45 to 55 minutes. If necessary, cover the lasagna with foil to prevent too much browning. Allow the lasagna to rest for 10 minutes. Garnish with additional basil.

CHICKEN *and* SPINACH LASAGNA

SERVES 8

A green salad and crusty bread are the only accompaniments needed to enjoy this four cheese chicken lasagna.
Lasagnas make hearty gifts, one dish meals that can be enjoyed immediately or easily saved for later.

1 cup ricotta cheese
¾ cup cottage cheese
10 ounces frozen spinach, thawed and drained
1 egg
1½ teaspoons chopped fresh oregano
⅓ cup olive oil
1 medium onion, chopped
2 large cloves garlic, sliced
28 ounces canned Italian whole peeled tomatoes

6 ounces canned tomato paste
¾ cup water
4 to 6 fresh basil leaves, chopped
2 tablespoons sugar
coarse salt and freshly ground pepper
9 lasagna noodles, cooked and drained
4 chicken breast halves, cooked and cubed
1 cup crumbled feta cheese
1½ cups shredded mozzarella cheese

Preheat the oven to 375°F. Combine the ricotta cheese, cottage cheese, spinach, egg and oregano in a medium bowl. Cover and refrigerate until ready to use. Heat the olive oil in a medium heavy saucepan over medium-low and sauté the onions and garlic for 8 to 10 minutes. Mix in the tomatoes, tomato paste, water and basil. Blend the ingredients with a potato masher or hand blender until chunky. Mix in the sugar; season with salt and pepper. Bring the sauce to a boil, then reduce heat and allow to simmer for 15 minutes. Rinse the lasagna noodles with cold water and drain again. Lightly oil a 9 by 13-inch baking pan. To assemble the lasagna, spoon 1 cup of the pasta sauce over the bottom of the pan. Arrange 3 lasagna noodles over the sauce. Top the noodles with 1 cup of the sauce, followed by half of the chicken, ⅓ cup of the feta and ½ cup of the mozzarella. Layer 3 more noodles, followed by 1 cup of the sauce, the remaining chicken, all of the reserved ricotta mixture, ⅓ cup of the feta and ½ cup of the mozzarella. Layer the remaining noodles, sauce, feta and mozzarella. Cover the lasagna loosely with foil and bake for 45 minutes. Remove the foil for the last 5 minutes of baking. Allow the lasagna to rest for 10 minutes before serving.

from

he sea

menu sampler

BACKYARD BASH

Cold Boiled Shrimp

Fish Tacos with Tropical Fruit Salsa

Cilantro Lime Summer Corn Salad

Refried White Beans

Frozen Margarita Pie

Rosé Wine Freezes

EAST MEETS WEST

Minced Pork in Lettuce Cups

Sautéed Broccoli Rabe

Sesame Citrus Sea Bass

Basmati Rice

Coconut Lime Rice Pudding

Lychee Martini

SEASIDE SUPPER

Southwestern Shrimp Fritters with
Chili Ginger Sauce

Crab Cakes with Avocado Salsa

Italian Seafood Stew

Tomato and Asparagus Salad
with Champagne Vinaigrette

Blackberry Raspberry Crisp

Citrus Mint Granitas

seaside supper

seaside supper

There is something about the
seashore that makes get-togethers
more inviting, friends (and rules)
more relaxed, and sends cares
vanishing over the endless horizon.
The day's catch is served up with
summer favorites on a weather-
washed table. People come to
the table barefoot, and somehow
dinner tastes all the better for it.
Well after the sun has set on this
long lazy day, the peaceful rhythm
of the waves stays with you.

*Tomato and Asparagus Salad
with Champagne Vinaigrette,* PAGE 121

Italian Seafood Stew, PAGE 157

Crab Cakes with Avocado Salsa, PAGE 153
Southwestern Shrimp Fritters with Chili Ginger Sauce, PAGE 61

seaside supper

DETAILS

Invitations
Vintage bottles bear messages of
welcome to friends—those long lost
and those close by.

Favors
Monogrammed totes filled with
beach towels and toys are a piece of
summer to take home.

For Fun
Creativity gets competitive as
guests vie for the coveted *Best Sandcastle*
trophy, then team up for a seashell
scavenger hunt at low tide.

seaside supper

TIPS

Use shells, sea glass and other treasures to adorn a simple table and let the ocean be your backdrop.

Offer iced lemon towels as a refreshing way to cool down and clean off the sand before dinner.

Tubs of chilled, non-alcoholic drinks keep guests cool and hydrated.

Let the sound of the waves serve as background music or set up outdoor speakers to play everyone's favorite beach tunes.

Arrange comfortable chairs (and a basket of colorful sarongs if the sea breeze is cool) to enjoy the summer sunset.

CRAB CAKES *with* AVOCADO SALSA
MAKES 16 LARGE CRAB CAKES
Turn this main dish favorite into cocktail fare by forming about two dozen smaller cakes.

Crab Cakes:
2 pounds lump crabmeat
½ cup minced green onions
½ cup diced pimientos
½ cup mayonnaise
3 egg yolks, lightly beaten
½ teaspoon cayenne pepper
⅛ teaspoon coarse salt
freshly ground pepper
2½ cups fresh bread crumbs, divided
⅓ cup vegetable oil

Avocado Salsa:
2 large avocados, pitted, peeled and diced
½ cup minced red onion
1 tablespoon finely chopped fresh tarragon
4 tablespoons fresh lime juice
1 teaspoon coarse salt
freshly ground pepper

This recipe requires advance preparation. Line a large rimmed baking sheet with parchment paper. Combine the crabmeat, green onions, pimientos, mayonnaise, egg yolks, cayenne, salt and pepper in a large bowl. Add 1 cup of the bread crumbs and mix well. Form the crab mixture into 16 4 to 5-inch cakes. Coat the crab cakes with the remaining bread crumbs. Place on the baking sheet, cover and refrigerate until firm, about 3 hours. Meanwhile, gently combine the avocados, onions, tarragon, lime juice and salt in a medium bowl. Season with pepper, cover and refrigerate. Heat the vegetable oil in a skillet over medium-high. Sauté the crab cakes until golden on both sides. Transfer to a paper towel-lined plate to drain. Serve the crab cakes with the *Avocado Salsa.*

MUSSELS *with* GARLIC WHITE WINE SAUCE

SERVES 4 *to* 6
Not one drop of this flavorful cooking sauce should go to waste. Serve these mussels with crusty French bread or in the Belgian tradition with a heaping portion of Pommes Frites (page 215).

10 tablespoons butter
6 shallots, thinly sliced
4 cloves garlic, thinly sliced
2 stalks celery, sliced thinly crosswise
8 fresh thyme sprigs
1 to 1½ cups dry white wine

6 tablespoons crème fraîche
2 teaspoons freshly ground white pepper
2 pounds mussels, rinsed and cleaned
¼ cup chopped fresh Italian flat leaf parsley

Melt the butter in a Dutch oven over low heat. Add the shallots, garlic, celery and thyme, and sauté for 10 to 15 minutes or until soft. Add the wine, crème fraîche and white pepper. Increase heat and bring to a boil. Add the mussels, stir and cover. Cook 3 to 4 minutes, or until the mussels open. Discard any unopened mussels. Add the parsley and stir. Ladle the mussels and a generous amount of sauce into individual serving bowls.

◦ MUSSELS ◦

Take mussels home on ice in a bag that is not completely sealed. Cook them within 4 to 6 hours, keeping them refrigerated until ready to use. (You must discard any mussels that are open before cooking or unopened after cooking, so buy more than you need.) To prepare mussels, first scrub under cold running water with a stiff-bristled brush to remove sand and dirt from the shells. Next, get rid of the byssal threads, or "debeard," by grabbing the fibers and pulling firmly toward the hinged point of the shell.

HERB CRUSTED TILAPIA *with* TOMATO CHIVE BEURRE BLANC

SERVES 6

Japanese-style bread crumbs (panko) are more crisp and airy than traditional bread crumbs.
If your grocery store does not have it, panko can usually be found at Asian markets and gourmet food stores.

Herb Crusted Tilapia:
1½ cups panko bread crumbs
2 tablespoons snipped fresh chives
2 tablespoons chopped fresh parsley
2 eggs
2 tablespoons milk
6 tilapia fillets (about 3 pounds)
3 tablespoons olive oil

Tomato Chive Buerre Blanc:
½ cup dry white wine
½ cup heavy whipping cream
8 tablespoons (1 stick) butter, room temperature
1 tablespoon snipped fresh chives
1 medium tomato, seeded and diced
2 tablespoons chopped fresh thyme
2 tablespoons chopped fresh basil
1 teaspoon coarse salt
1 teaspoon freshly ground pepper
chopped fresh parsley, for garnish

Preheat the oven to 350°F. Lightly oil a baking sheet. Combine the panko and herbs in a wide shallow dish. Whisk together the eggs and milk in a separate wide shallow dish. Dip only one side of each fillet into the egg mixture. Place the fillet, egg side down, into the panko mixture, pressing gently so that the crumbs will adhere. Heat the olive oil in large skillet over medium-high. Sauté the fillets, breaded side down, until golden brown. Cook the fillets in batches, adding more olive oil as needed. Place the cooked fillets, breaded side up, on the prepared baking sheet. Bake the fillets in the oven for 8 to 10 minutes or until the fish flakes easily with a fork.

While the fish is baking, heat the wine in a medium saucepan over medium-high; reduce the wine to approximately 1 tablespoon or until almost dry, watching closely. Add the cream and reduce the mixture by half. Remove from heat and whisk in the butter, adding 1 tablespoon at a time, until incorporated. Add the chives, tomatoes, thyme, basil, salt and pepper. Serve the fillets over the *Tomato Chive Buerre Blanc* and garnish with parsley.

PAN SEARED TILAPIA *with* HONEY-JALAPEÑO VINAIGRETTE

SERVES 6

If tilapia is not available, other flaky white fish like catfish, freshwater bass or red snapper will work as well.

2 tablespoons apple cider vinegar
2 tablespoons chopped white or red onion
¼ teaspoon coarse salt
1 teaspoon plus ¼ cup olive oil, divided
1 to 2 medium jalapeños
1 tablespoon honey

1 tablespoon chopped fresh cilantro
1 clove garlic, finely minced
1 tablespoon Dijon mustard
freshly ground pepper
6 tilapia fillets (about 5 to 6 ounces each)

Combine the vinegar and onions in a small bowl; season with the salt and let stand for 10 minutes. Heat 1 teaspoon of the olive oil in a small skillet over medium-high. Add the whole jalapeños and cook, turning, until charred on all sides, about 3 to 5 minutes. Cool slightly and remove the charred skin; stem, seed and finely chop the jalapeños. Whisk the jalapeños, honey, cilantro, garlic, mustard and remaining ¼ cup of the olive oil into the reserved vinegar-onion mixture. Season the vinaigrette with salt and pepper. Lightly oil a large nonstick skillet and heat over high. Season the fillets with salt and pepper, and sear for 6 to 8 minutes, turning once, until opaque throughout. Transfer the fish to a platter. Whisk the vinaigrette and spoon over the fish.

SOUTHWESTERN SHRIMP *and* GRITS

SERVES 4

This dish has all the appeal of the traditional Southern staple with the addition of bold and spicy flavors.

Grits:
1 cup uncooked quick grits
1 cup shredded cheddar cheese
2 tablespoons butter

Shrimp:
1 tablespoon ground cumin
2 teaspoons ancho chile powder
½ teaspoon cayenne pepper
½ teaspoon coarse salt
¼ teaspoon freshly ground pepper

1 pound medium shrimp, peeled and deveined
2 tablespoons olive oil
4 cloves garlic, minced
2 to 3 fresh jalapeños, seeded and thinly sliced
¾ cup sliced fresh mushrooms
5 to 6 medium tomatoes, seeded and chopped
8 green onions (white and pale green parts only),
    thinly sliced on the diagonal, plus additional
6 slices bacon, cooked and crumbled
1½ tablespoons fresh lime juice
½ cup chicken broth

Cook the grits according to package directions. Add the cheese and butter to the cooked grits, and stir to combine. Set aside and keep warm. Combine the cumin, chile powder, cayenne, salt and pepper in a medium bowl. Add the shrimp and toss to coat. Heat the olive oil in a large skillet over medium. Add the shrimp, any of the extra spice mixture and the garlic. Sauté until the shrimp turn pink and are cooked through; remove to a bowl and set aside. Add the jalapeños, mushrooms and tomatoes to the skillet, and cook for 5 to 10 minutes. Stir in the shrimp, green onions and bacon, and cook for 1 minute. Add the lime juice and broth, and heat through. Serve the shrimp over the grits and garnish with the additional sliced green onions.

CILANTRO LIME SHRIMP

SERVES 4 *to* 5

This is a quick meal for busy weeknights or effortless entertaining.

½ cup olive oil
3 cloves garlic, pressed
1 teaspoon dried thyme
¼ cup chopped fresh cilantro
½ jalapeño, seeded and minced
1 teaspoon paprika
1 teaspoon coarse salt
1 teaspoon brown sugar

1 teaspoon ground cumin
1 teaspoon Worcestershire sauce
½ teaspoon cayenne pepper
½ teaspoon crushed red pepper
juice of 2 limes

1½ to 2 pounds large shrimp, peeled and deveined
1 cup rice, cooked according to package directions

Whisk together all the ingredients except the shrimp and rice in a medium bowl. Add the shrimp to the mixture and marinate in the refrigerator for 30 minutes to 1 hour. Place the shrimp and marinade in a skillet, and cook over medium-high heat until the shrimp turn pink, about 5 minutes. Serve over rice.

GRILLED TUSCAN SHRIMP *with* LEMON ORZO

SERVES 6

No matter the name—brochettes in France, spiedini in Italy, satay in Asia or
shish kebab in Turkey—food on a stick is universally popular. If you use wooden skewers,
remember to soak them in water for at least 30 minutes first to prevent burning.

Tuscan Shrimp:
¼ cup olive oil
¼ cup fresh lemon juice
1 teaspoon coarse salt
¼ teaspoon freshly ground pepper
1 teaspoon dry mustard
2 teaspoons Dijon mustard
3 cloves garlic, lightly crushed
1 medium onion, diced
½ cup Tuscan peppers (also known as banana,
   pepperoncini or golden Greek peppers), chopped
½ cup minced fresh parsley

¼ cup minced fresh basil
2 pounds shrimp, peeled and deveined
6 skewers

Lemon Orzo:
1 pound orzo pasta
¼ cup olive oil
zest of 3 large lemons, finely grated
juice of 3 large lemons
⅛ teaspoon coarse salt
¼ cup freshly grated Parmigiano-Reggiano cheese
freshly ground pepper

This recipe requires advance preparation. Whisk together the olive oil, lemon juice, salt, pepper and mustards in a medium bowl. Stir in the garlic, onions, peppers, parsley and basil. Add the shrimp and toss to coat. Cover and refrigerate for 2 to 3 hours. Cook and drain the orzo according to package instructions. Place the orzo in a bowl, add the olive oil and let cool to room temperature. Add the lemon zest, juice and salt to the orzo. Stir in the cheese and season with pepper. Preheat the grill to medium-high. Remove the shrimp from the marinade and thread onto the skewers, through the head and tail. Discard the marinade. Grill for 2 to 3 minutes per side or until the shrimp turn pink. Serve over the *Lemon Orzo*.

SAVORY SHRIMP *with* TOMATOES *and* AVOCADOS

SERVES 4

This dish is a happy combination of three summer favorites.

2 tablespoons butter
4 tablespoons olive oil
5 cloves garlic, minced
1½ pounds shrimp, peeled and deveined
¼ cup white wine
1 cup cherry tomatoes, halved

1 tablespoon chopped fresh basil
1 tablespoon chopped fresh oregano
1 tablespoon chopped fresh Italian flat leaf parsley
coarse salt and freshly ground pepper
1 avocado, pitted, peeled and diced
1 cup rice, cooked according to package directions

Melt the butter in a large sauté pan over medium heat; add the olive oil. Sauté the garlic for 1 minute and add the shrimp. Sauté the shrimp until pink. Add the wine, tomatoes and herbs, and season with salt and pepper. Remove from heat and gently stir in the avocados. Serve over the rice.

SEAFOOD GUMBO

COURTESY *of* GOODE COMPANY SEAFOOD

SERVES 12 *to* 14

Toasted garlic bread is the perfect accompaniment to this hearty gumbo. This recipe can easily be doubled to serve a crowd.

½ cup vegetable oil
½ cup all-purpose flour
1 cup chopped celery
2 cups chopped onions
1 cup chopped bell peppers
2 tablespoons chopped fresh garlic
1½ teaspoons chopped fresh thyme
4 dried bay leaves
½ cup tomato paste

½ teaspoon cayenne pepper
3 quarts seafood stock
1 pound crab claw meat
1½ pounds small shrimp, boiled and peeled
24 lightly sautéed oysters
gumbo filé, for garnish
diced green onions, for garnish

Heat the oil in a large stockpot over medium-high until hot but not smoking. Gradually whisk in the flour. Cook for 20 minutes or until the roux is the color of peanut butter, whisking constantly. Add the celery, onions and bell peppers. Cook for 10 to 20 minutes or until the vegetables are tender; the roux will cool slightly as the vegetables are added and darken as the vegetables release their natural sugars. Stir in the garlic, thyme, bay leaves, tomato paste and cayenne. Cook for 5 to 10 minutes or until heated through, stirring occasionally. Add the seafood stock. Bring to a boil and reduce the heat to medium. Simmer for 5 to 10 minutes, skimming the surface. Add the crab, shrimp and oysters. Discard the bay leaves. Garnish with filé and green onions.

ITALIAN SEAFOOD STEW

SERVES 2

*This old world stew is as striking as it is flavorful. For a more substantial meal,
serve it over linguine with plenty of crusty bread to mop up the sauce.*

½ cup olive oil
1 shallot, diced
2 to 3 cloves garlic, minced
2 Anaheim peppers, seeded and chopped
1 pint (2 cups) cherry tomatoes
2 cups chopped fresh Italian flat leaf parsley
coarse salt
cayenne pepper

1 thread saffron
¾ cup dry vermouth or white wine
12 Little Neck clams, scrubbed
12 black mussels, scrubbed and beards removed
1 lobster tail (6 to 8 ounces)
1 tilapia fillet, washed and halved
6 large shrimp, shelled and deveined

Heat the olive oil in a heavy stockpot over medium-low. Add the shallots, garlic and peppers, and sauté for about 10 minutes. Add the tomatoes and parsley, and season with salt and cayenne; cook for 3 minutes. Add the saffron, vermouth and ½ cup of water; bring to a boil. Add the clams, mussels, lobster and tilapia, and cover tightly. Steam until the clams and mussels open, about 5 to 8 minutes. Add the shrimp, cover and steam for 2 more minutes. Remove from heat and set aside for 2 minutes. Transfer the seafood with a slotted spoon to soup bowls and ladle in the remaining broth.

157

FISH TACOS *with* TROPICAL FRUIT SALSA

MAKES 16 TACOS

Rice and black beans complement this light and spicy dish.

Tropical Fruit Salsa:
1 cup peeled, pitted and diced mango (about 1 mango)
1 cup peeled, cored and diced pineapple
2 avocados, pitted, peeled and diced
¼ cup chopped fresh cilantro, plus additional
¼ cup minced red onion
1 jalapeño, seeded and minced
2 tablespoons fresh lime juice
coarse salt and freshly ground pepper

Tacos:
1 tablespoon fresh lime juice
4 tablespoons vegetable oil, divided
coarse salt and freshly ground pepper
¼ cup chopped green onions
2 pounds skinless, boneless red snapper fillets,
   cut into ½-inch pieces
3 canned chipotle chiles in adobo sauce, finely chopped
3 cups thinly shredded cabbage
16 corn tortillas
Cilantro Crème Fraîche (recipe below) or sour cream

Gently mix together the salsa ingredients in a medium bowl. Season with salt and pepper, and set aside. Whisk together the lime juice and 3 tablespoons of the oil in a small bowl. Season with salt and pepper, and set the dressing aside. Heat the remaining 1 tablespoon of oil in a large sauté pan over medium-high. Add the onions and sauté until translucent. Season the fish with salt and pepper, and add to the onions. Sauté, stirring frequently, about 3 to 4 minutes or until just cooked through. Remove the pan from heat, add the chiles and mix gently. Toss the cabbage together with the dressing in a medium bowl. Warm the tortillas in a skillet and fill each with the fish mixture, cabbage and *Tropical Fruit Salsa*. Top with the *Cilantro Crème Fraîche*.

158

> ❧ CILANTRO CRÈME FRAÎCHE ❧
>
> ½ cup buttermilk
> juice of 2 limes
> 1 serrano chile, minced
> 1 bunch cilantro, chopped (save sprigs for garnish)
> 3 cups crème fraîche
> ½ teaspoon ground cumin
>
> In a blender, purée the buttermilk, lime juice, chiles and cilantro. Transfer the mixture to a bowl and fold in the crème fraîche and cumin.

SEAFOOD PEPPER POT

SERVES 8 *to* 10

This intense and spicy stew-like soup is reminiscent of the flavors of Louisiana.
It can be prepared with any mild and relatively firm fish like tilapia or snapper.

¼ pound bacon, cut into 2-inch pieces
1 pound fresh okra, sliced (optional)
1 red bell pepper, seeded and chopped
1 green bell pepper, seeded and chopped
1 large onion, chopped
6 cloves garlic, minced
28 ounces canned diced tomatoes, undrained
1 fresh jalapeño, seeded and chopped

4 teaspoons chopped fresh thyme
4 bay leaves
1 teaspoon crushed red pepper
3 tablespoons bottled clam juice
2 cups chicken broth
2 pounds cod, cut into 2-inch pieces
1 pound bay scallops
2 pounds shrimp, shelled and deveined

Cook the bacon in a heavy stockpot over medium-high heat until lightly browned. Reduce heat to medium and add the okra, peppers, onions and garlic, and sauté until the vegetables are soft. Add the tomatoes, jalapeños, thyme, bay leaves, red pepper, clam juice and broth, and stir to combine. Simmer, partially covered, for 30 minutes. Add the fish and scallops, and cook over medium heat for 5 minutes. Add the shrimp and cook until pink, about 2 to 3 minutes.

Fish Tacos with Tropical Fruit Salsa, PAGE 158

Seared Sesame Tuna, PAGE 161

SEARED SESAME TUNA

SERVES 2

True wasabi is a highly prized root once grown only in Japan. It is most commonly found in a paste or powder form,
but can sometimes be found fresh. Its complex, pungent flavor is a delicious complement to fish.

1 cup teriyaki sauce
¼ cup honey
¼ cup Dijon mustard
1½ teaspoons powdered wasabi, sifted
2 cloves garlic, slightly crushed

1 to 2 tablespoons peeled and grated fresh ginger
2 sushi grade tuna steaks (½ to ¾-inch thick),
    rinsed and patted dry (about 4 to 6 ounces each)
1 tablespoon olive oil
sesame seeds

Mix together the teriyaki sauce, honey, mustard, wasabi, garlic and ginger in a medium bowl. Add the tuna steaks and marinate for 1 hour. Heat the olive oil in a skillet over medium-high. Remove the tuna from the marinade and lightly sprinkle with sesame seeds, gently pressing the seeds onto the steaks. Cook for 30 to 45 seconds per side or until the sesame seeds are golden brown.

SESAME CITRUS SEA BASS

SERVES 4

Wonderful for dinner parties or weeknight dinners, this dish is both sophisticated and easy to make.
Complete the meal with sushi rice and your favorite green vegetable sautéed with sesame oil, garlic and crushed red pepper.

1 tablespoon olive oil
2 tablespoons fresh lime juice
2 tablespoons freshly squeezed orange juice
2 tablespoons chopped fresh cilantro
1 teaspoon chopped fresh mint
2 tablespoons peeled and minced fresh ginger

2 tablespoons minced shallots
2 tablespoons sesame oil
coarse salt and freshly ground pepper
4 sea bass fillets (about 6 ounces each)

Preheat the oven to 500°F. Coat an ovenproof dish with the olive oil and set aside. Mix together the lime juice, orange juice, cilantro, mint, ginger, shallots and sesame oil in a small bowl. Season with salt and pepper. Place the fish in the prepared dish, turning to coat with the olive oil. Season the fish with salt and pepper, and pour ½ tablespoon of the sesame citrus sauce over each fillet. Roast for about 12 to 15 minutes or until opaque in the center. Serve topped with the remaining sauce.

✑ GINGER ✎

Look for hard ginger roots with smooth skin—wrinkles are a sign of age. A 1-inch piece typically yields about 1 tablespoon of minced ginger. Scrape the ginger with the side of a spoon to peel it without taking off too much flesh (the skin is thin and scrapes off easily). To keep tiny fibers from clogging your grater, try an all-porcelain grater or one made of bamboo strips. Always grate ginger in a circular motion.

FILETTOS *de* TONNO

COURTESY *of* EFISIO FARRIS, CHEF *and* OWNER, ARCODORO *and* POMODORO

SERVES 4

According to Chef Farris, "I come from a land of shepherds, but seafood is my real passion.
I crave this famly-style dish made from the freshest summer ingredients, and the tuna's flavorful and less expensive dark meat."

¼ cup extra virgin olive oil, plus more for searing
2 pounds yellowfin tuna steaks, cut into 8 pieces
4 cloves garlic, thinly sliced
6 anchovies
½ cup white wine
1 bunch green onions, white part only, thinly sliced

1 cup Italian longhorn peppers (or banana peppers),
   seeded and julienned
2 cups teardrop tomatoes (or cherry tomatoes), halved
juice of 1 lemon
½ bunch fresh Italian flat leaf parsley, finely chopped
3 sprigs fresh oregano, leaves only, chopped

Coat bottom of a large sauté pan with a thin layer of olive oil. Place pan over medium-high heat until oil is smoking hot. Place tuna pieces into the pan and sear both sides about 30 seconds per side. Remove tuna pieces from heat and set aside. In another sauté pan, heat the ¼ cup of olive oil over medium-high. Add garlic and heat until golden. Add anchovies to the pan and stir until dissolved. Pour in the wine and cook until alcohol evaporates. Stir in green onions, peppers and tomatoes, and toss well. Stir in lemon juice, parsley and oregano, and combine well. Add the tuna and season to taste. Reduce heat to medium and cook for about 5 minutes or until tuna is cooked to desired doneness. Serve tuna and vegetables drizzled with the sauce.

SNAPPER SHERIDAN

COURTESY *of* TONY VALLONE, TONY'S

SERVES 4

Signature recipes, the stock in trade of any great restaurant, are not often found in cookbooks. But here,
Tony Vallone reveals his secret for a dish he describes as "delicate and spring-fresh."

½ cup fresh lemon juice
½ cup white wine
¼ cup heavy whipping cream
1 shallot, minced
½ pound (2 sticks) unsalted butter, cold, cubed
coarse salt and freshly ground pepper
3 eggs
1 cup freshly grated Parmigiano-Reggiano cheese
8 skinless snapper scaloppine (about 2 ounces each)

1 cup all-purpose flour
½ cup canola oil
4 tablespoons (½ stick) butter
6 white mushrooms, cleaned and sliced
1 cup green peas, cooked
1 yellow pepper, roasted, peeled, seeded and julienned
1 red pepper, roasted, peeled, seeded and julienned

In a small pot over medium heat, reduce the lemon juice, white wine and cream with the shallots, keeping the mixture at a low boil. Stirring frequently, reduce the mixture by two-thirds or until a heavy sauce-like consistency is achieved, about 30 minutes. Remove from heat and add the butter, one cube at a time, whisking constantly and not adding more butter until the previous cube is melted, approximately 40 minutes. While incorporating the butter, return the pot to very low heat as needed to warm the sauce. Season with salt and pepper.

Whisk together the eggs with the cheese; set aside. Dredge the fish in the flour, shaking to remove the excess. Heat the canola oil in a 9-inch Teflon®-coated sauté pan until the oil sizzles when flour is sprinkled above the oil. Dip the fish in the egg-cheese mixture and place directly in the oil. Cook on both sides until golden brown. Remove from the oil and place on a rack to allow the oil to drain from the fish.

Add the butter to the sauté pan and heat until melted. Sauté the mushrooms until desired doneness. Toss with the peas and peppers until heated through. Place the hot fish on a plate, top with the mushroom-pepper mixture and ladle the sauce on top.

BROILED HALIBUT *with* MEYER LEMON SAUCE

SERVES 6

This entrée takes just minutes to prepare, so the kitchen stays cooler on summer nights.
It is delicious served warm or chilled. If you use plain whole milk yogurt (not Greek), drain it in a colander
lined with a double thickness of paper towels and chill for 1 hour before preparing the sauce.

Fish:
extra virgin olive oil
6 halibut fillets (about 6 ounces each), without skin,
  rinsed and patted dry
coarse salt and freshly ground pepper

Meyer Lemon Sauce:
1 cup Greek or plain yogurt
1 teaspoon finely grated Meyer lemon zest
1 teaspoon fresh Meyer lemon juice
1 teaspoon finely grated lime zest
1 teaspoon fresh lime juice
¾ teaspoon coarse salt
½ teaspoon honey

Preheat the oven to broil and set the oven rack at the highest position. Lightly coat the rack of a broiler pan with olive oil. Season the halibut with salt and pepper. Broil for 10 to 14 minutes, turning halfway through, or until the fish flakes easily when tested with a fork. While the fish is cooking, whisk together the sauce ingredients plus 2 tablespoons of water in a small bowl. Serve the halibut with the *Meyer Lemon Sauce.*

SALMON *with* HORSERADISH SAUCE

SERVES 6

With a little easy work up front, this meal is ready to serve in 15 minutes.
The horseradish lends a kick to both the salmon and the sauce.

163

Horseradish Sauce:
½ cup mayonnaise
¼ cup sour cream
2 tablespoons chopped fresh basil
2 tablespoons prepared horseradish
1 tablespoon soy sauce
1 teaspoon fresh lemon juice

Fish:
6 king salmon fillets (about 6 ounces each)
3 tablespoons extra virgin olive oil
2 tablespoons prepared horseradish
1 tablespoon soy sauce
1 clove garlic, minced

Whisk together the sauce ingredients in a small bowl and refrigerate for 1 to 2 hours. Place the fish in a lightly oiled baking dish. Combine the olive oil, horseradish, soy sauce and garlic in a small bowl, and brush onto the fillets. Cover the fish and marinate for 1 to 2 hours in the refrigerator. Preheat the oven to 425°F. Bake the fish for 15 minutes or until desired doneness. Serve with the *Horseradish Sauce.*

> ∾ BUYING FRESH FISH ∾
>
> *Fish should never smell "fishy"—it should smell like the water*
> *it was swimming in, whether fresh or salty. The flesh of fish*
> *should feel firm to the touch; find whole fish with clear (not*
> *cloudy) eyes. It is best to use seafood the same day you buy*
> *it. Have the fish packed on ice and keep it in the refrigerator*
> *until you are ready to use.*

Poached Salmon in Thai Green Curry Broth, PAGE 165

POACHED SALMON *in* THAI GREEN CURRY BROTH

SERVES 2 *to* 4

Do not be daunted by the list of ingredients—they combine to create a sublime and intensely flavored broth.
When you choose lemongrass, look for fresh, fragrant stalks and avoid any that look dry or brown. The entire stalk is edible.
Try serving this dish over steamed jasmine rice to soak up the delicious broth.

1 tablespoon vegetable oil
4 tablespoons coriander seed
¾ teaspoon cumin seed, crushed
2 cloves garlic, minced
½ cup coarsely chopped fresh shallots
3 tablespoons finely chopped fresh lemongrass
   (only use the bottom 4 inches of the stalks)
1 to 2 serrano chiles, seeded and thinly sliced
2 tablespoons peeled and finely grated fresh ginger
2 green onions (white and pale green parts only),
   thinly sliced
1 pinch ground turmeric

3 tablespoons fresh lime juice
zest of 1 lime, finely grated
3½ cups chicken broth
1 teaspoon coarse salt
¼ teaspoon freshly ground pepper
1 pound skinless salmon, bones removed
   and cut into 1-inch pieces
3 cups fresh spinach leaves, coarsely chopped
2 tablespoons coarsely chopped fresh cilantro
1 tablespoon coarsely chopped fresh basil
1 tablespoon coarsely chopped fresh mint

Heat the oil in a medium saucepan over medium. Add the coriander and cumin, and cook for 1 minute. Add the garlic, shallots, lemongrass, chiles, ginger, onions, turmeric, lime juice and zest, and cook for 3 to 4 minutes or until softened. Add the broth, salt and pepper. Bring to a simmer and cook for 30 minutes. Pour the mixture through a fine sieve into a clean saucepan; discard the solids. Bring the broth to a simmer, add the salmon and cook for 2 to 5 minutes or until done. Stir in the spinach and herbs, and cook until the greens are wilted. Serve immediately.

165

OVEN ROASTED BOURBON SALMON

SERVES 8

The brown sugar and bourbon-based marinade gives the salmon its delicate, interestingly Asian flavor.
This entrée can also be grilled, but leave skin on to protect the delicate flesh and help the fish maintain its shape.
Brown the presentation side of the fish first, then finish with the skin side down.

Marinade:
¾ cup packed brown sugar
⅓ cup bourbon
¼ cup soy sauce
2 tablespoons fresh lime juice
2 teaspoons peeled and grated fresh ginger
¼ teaspoon freshly ground pepper
2 cloves garlic, crushed

Fish:
8 skinless salmon fillets (about 6 ounces each)
¼ cup thinly sliced green onions
4 teaspoons sesame seeds, toasted

Combine the marinade ingredients in a large resealable plastic bag; add the salmon fillets (check for bones). Seal the bag and marinate in the refrigerator for 30 minutes, turning once. Preheat the oven to 400°F. Line a baking dish with aluminum foil and lightly brush the foil with oil. Remove the fillets from the marinade and place in the prepared baking dish; discard the marinade. Roast in the oven for 15 to 18 minutes or until the fish flakes easily when tested with a fork. Sprinkle each fillet with the green onions and sesame seeds.

main c

ourses

menu sampler

TODAY'S SPECIAL

*Pork Chops with
Potatoes and Onions*

*Lemony Green Beans
and Mushrooms*

Apple Cranberry Galette

SUNDAY NIGHT DINNER

*Butter Lettuce, Pomegranate
and Walnut Salad*

Coq au Vin with Currants and Figs

Balsamic Glazed Carrots

Chocolate Molten Lava Cakes

HOLIDAY GATHERING

Champagne Pomegranate Punch

*Pancetta Medallions with
Goat Cheese and Pear*

*Cranberry Salsa with
Warm Brie and Pistachios*

Pumpkin Mushroom Soup

*Herb Crusted Standing Rib Roast
with Cherry Port Sauce*

Beet and Blood Orange Salad

Brussels Sprouts with Prosciutto

French Onion Bread Pudding

Big as Texas Brandy Apple Pie

Cranberry Cheesecake

*Chocolate Pots du Crème with
Peppermint Whipped Cream*

holiday gathering

Cranberry Salsa with Warm Brie and Pistachios, PAGE 54

holiday gathering

The holiday season is, above all, a time of anticipation: parties, gifts and—of course—The Family Feast. At no other time of the year do we so look forward to a single meal. Time-honored sentimental favorites grace the table, and an occasional new dish vies to become part of the tradition. It is a time of joyful merriment and celebration, a season that brings families and good friends together to connect.

holiday gathering

DETAILS

Invitations
A collage of children's artwork
and cut paper snowflakes delivers party
details along with a timeless spirit of
childlike anticipation.

Favors
Small loaves of *Sugar and Spice and
Everything Nice Loaf Bread* are a taste
of the season to enjoy back
home by the fire.

Décor
Gracefully doubling as placecards,
a table full of small paperwhites is a
subtle reminder that winter is also
a time of growth and renewal.

Cranberry Cheesecake, PAGE 243

Chocolate Pots du Crème with Peppermint Whipped Cream, PAGE 244

holiday gathering

TIPS

Set the table well in advance
and label all serving pieces, cutting
down on the day's tasks and
eliminating last minute "making do."

Include well-loved
family favorites and at least one
unexpected dish that might just
become a new tradition.

Make the kids table
special with thoughtful settings
and fun activities.

Tins, boxes and other festive
containers labeled with holiday
wishes are good for sharing
leftovers with family and friends.

Grilled Lamb with Savory Mint Relish, PAGE 189

GRILLED LAMB *with* SAVORY MINT RELISH
SERVES 8

The zesty relish does all the work in this simple lamb recipe. Marinating the lamb in the relish for up to a day can intensify its flavor.
This relish is delicious on other grilled meats (like flank or flat iron steak, or Cornish game hens).

Savory Mint Relish:
¼ cup capers, soaked in water for 30 minutes,
   drained and coarsely chopped
½ cup chopped fresh Italian flat leaf parsley
⅓ cup chopped green onions
½ cup chopped fresh mint
½ cup fresh lemon juice
2 teaspoons grated lemon zest
1 cup extra virgin olive oil
1 teaspoon crushed red pepper

1½ teaspoons coarse salt
1½ teaspoons freshly ground pepper, divided

Lamb:
3 pound butterflied leg of lamb
3 cloves garlic, minced
1½ teaspoons salt
1 teaspoon freshly ground pepper
1 teaspoon crushed red pepper

Combine the relish ingredients in a medium bowl; set aside. Place the lamb in a baking dish. Combine the garlic, salt, pepper and red pepper; rub on the surface of the lamb. Pour ½ cup of the relish over the lamb, turning to coat evenly. Lightly oil the grill and preheat to medium-high. Grill the lamb until a meat thermometer reads 135°F, turning occasionally, about 20 to 25 minutes. Remove from the grill and let rest for 15 minutes. Thinly slice the lamb across the grain and arrange on a platter. Serve with the remaining *Savory Mint Relish*.

LAMB CHOPS PROVENÇAL
SERVES 4 *to* 6

These lamb chops are an imaginative and tasty alternative to everyday meat and potatoes.

189

3 tablespoons olive oil, divided
2 cups thinly sliced sweet onions
   (such as Vidalia or Texas 1015)
4 or 5 medium vine-ripened tomatoes,
   cut into ¼-inch slices, seeds removed
coarse salt and freshly ground pepper
½ teaspoon chopped fresh rosemary

½ teaspoon chopped fresh thyme
½ cup freshly grated Parmesan cheese
1½ pounds Yukon Gold potatoes,
   cut into ⅛-inch slices (unpeeled)
6 medium lamb chops, trimmed

Preheat the oven to 450°F. Lightly coat a 9 by 13-inch baking dish with cooking spray and set aside. Heat 2 tablespoons of the olive oil in a large skillet over medium-low. Add the onions and cook until translucent, stirring occasionally, about 5 minutes. Remove from heat and add the tomatoes and ¼ teaspoon salt. Stir to combine being careful not to break up the tomatoes.

In a small bowl, combine ¼ teaspoon salt, ⅛ teaspoon pepper, the herbs and the cheese. Spread half of the tomato and onion mixture in the bottom of the reserved baking dish; top with half of the potato slices. Sprinkle half of the herb mixture over the potatoes. Repeat the layers ending with the herb mixture. Cover the dish with foil and bake for 30 minutes.

Meanwhile, season the lamb chops with salt and pepper. Heat the remaining tablespoon of olive oil in a skillet over medium. Add the chops and brown, about 3 minutes per side. Remove the lamb chops from the skillet and add to the dish in the oven, placing on top of the potatoes. Remove and discard the foil. Continue cooking until the potatoes are fork tender and the cheese is lightly browned, about 10 to 12 minutes.

HERB CRUSTED STANDING RIB ROAST *with* CHERRY PORT SAUCE

SERVES 6 *to* 8

This is a showstopping rib roast for special occasions.
Black peppercorns (or a mix of pink and green) make an impressive and tasty crust.
The richly hued Cherry Port Sauce also complements duck or pork.

Rib Roast:
2 tablespoons coarse salt
1 tablespoon black peppercorns, cracked
3 cloves garlic
½ cup chopped shallots (about 2 large bulbs)
3 tablespoons chopped fresh thyme
3 tablespoons chopped fresh rosemary
½ cup olive oil
1 standing rib roast
  (about 8 pounds and 3 to 4 ribs), trimmed

Cherry Port Sauce:
½ cup frozen dark sweet cherries, thawed and halved
1 cup chicken broth
1 cup beef broth
½ cup port
1 sprig fresh thyme
1 teaspoon cornstarch
4 tablespoons (½ stick) butter, cut into ½-inch pieces,
  room temperature
coarse salt and freshly ground pepper

This recipe requires advance preparation. Combine the salt, peppercorns, garlic, shallots, thyme and rosemary in a small food processor; pulse to form a paste. With the machine running, slowly add the olive oil. Coat the entire roast with the olive oil mixture. Cover and marinate the meat in the refrigerator for 4 to 6 hours. Preheat the oven to 450°F with the baking rack positioned in the center of the oven. Allow the meat to come to room temperature, at least 1 hour. Place the meat in a large roasting pan and cook for 20 minutes. Reduce heat to 350°F and continue cooking until the temperature in the center of the roast registers 127°F, about 2½ hours. Transfer the meat to a platter and cover loosely with foil. Allow the meat to rest for 25 to 30 minutes.

Place the cherries, broth, port and thyme in a heavy saucepan and bring to a boil. Reduce heat and simmer until the mixture is reduced to ½ cup, about 15 minutes. Combine the cornstarch and 2 teaspoons of water in a small bowl and mix until smooth; add to the sauce and bring to a simmer, whisking constantly. Whisk in the butter, one piece at a time, until the butter is incorporated into the sauce. Season with salt and pepper. Carve the roast and serve with the warm *Cherry Port Sauce*.

190

✑ TIPS *for* ENTERTAINING ✑

Define the Event

- *Start with (or create) the reason for the gathering; is it a celebration, special occasion or holiday?*
- *How will you celebrate (dinner party, cocktails, brunch, lunch or backyard barbeque) and where?*
- *Carefully consider the guest list—some parties are right for mixing friends from different parts of your life.*
- *Invitations (written or verbal) should clearly convey purpose, place, time and dress.*
- *A good theme makes the event more interesting; it can also help guide planning decisions.*

Set the Scene

- *Ambience starts with first impressions; establish the mood and theme where guests arrive.*
- *Give seating some thought—a good seating plan helps stimulate dynamic connections.*

- *Centerpieces should be low so they do not obstruct conversation; lighting should be soft and flattering; use candles after dark and never scented ones at the table.*
- *Be creative with table décor, but stick to accepted rules when placing plates, flatware and stemware.*

Plan the Menu

- *Serve appetizers, but leave room for dinner.*
- *Create menus with make ahead steps, and pick up an appetizer or dessert (not everything has to be homemade).*
- *Build menus around fresh, seasonal ingredients.*
- *Keep the surprise in the party, not in the food. Test untried recipes in the kitchen, not on guests.*
- *A party's success depends less on food and décor than on the welcome you provide—remember this when things go wrong, which they sometimes do.*

Herb Crusted Standing Rib Roast with Cherry Port Sauce, PAGE 190

Congressional Chili, PAGE 193

CONGRESSIONAL CHILI

SERVES 8 *to* 10

The secret ingredient in this chili is red mole, a sauce first created in 1680 in Puebla, Mexico.
Jalapeño Cheese Biscuits (page 36) are exactly the right accompaniment for this award winning chili.

1 tablespoon olive oil
2 medium yellow onions, diced
2 green bell peppers, diced
2 cloves garlic, pressed
coarse salt and freshly ground pepper
2½ pounds ground beef, preferably sirloin
16 ounces canned tomato sauce

3 tablespoons prepared red mole
3 tablespoons chili powder
3 cups water
32 ounces canned kidney beans
shredded cheddar cheese
diced onions

Heat the olive oil in a large skillet over medium. Add the onions, peppers and garlic. Sauté until the onions are translucent and the peppers begin to soften. Season with salt and pepper and set aside. Brown the beef in a soup pot; drain off any excess fat. Add half of the sautéed onion-pepper mixture to the meat. Stir in the tomato sauce, mole, chili powder and water. Bring to a boil, reduce heat and simmer for 30 minutes. Adjust the seasonings by adding additional salt, pepper, mole or chili powder. Simmer for 30 minutes. Add the beans and the remaining half of the onion-pepper mixture; cook for 15 minutes. Serve topped with cheese and onions.

"THE CHURRASCO" BEEF TENDERLOIN

COURTESY *of* CHEF MICHAEL CORDÚA, CORDÚA RESTAURANT GROUP

SERVES 6

This signature dish is Cordúa's most requested menu item. It is delicious served with plantain chips,
using leftover Chimichurri Sauce as a dip, and Cilantro Rice (page 214). Leftover beef tenderloin can be frozen for another day.

Chimichurri Sauce:
3 bunches curly parsley, chopped
6 tablespoons chopped fresh garlic (about 16 cloves)
2 cups extra virgin olive oil
1 cup white vinegar
coarse salt and freshly ground pepper

The Churrasco:
1 beef tenderloin, center cut
coarse salt and freshly ground pepper

Chimichurri Sauce: Combine all the ingredients in a food processor and let sit for at least 2 hours before serving.

The Churrasco: Trim away all the visible fat and gristle from the beef tenderloin; cut out a 4-inch portion from the center. Make a half-turn with center cut portion. Make a cut along the 4-inch side parallel to cutting board and continue to cut in a jelly-roll fashion so that you are "rolling out" the steak. When finished, it should be a rectangular piece of meat, about ¼-inch thick. Add salt and pepper to taste; baste with *Chimichurri Sauce.* Grill on a very hot fire to desired degree of doneness. Serve with additional *Chimichurri Sauce* on the side.

BRAISED SHORT RIBS

SERVES 6 *to* 8

Slow cooking but worth the wait, this hearty entrée is wonderful with mashed potatoes or creamy polenta
and sweet English peas. If you use bone-in short ribs, be sure to drain the grease.

¼ cup plus 1 tablespoon olive oil, divided
4 to 4½ pounds boneless beef short ribs, trimmed
coarse salt and freshly ground pepper
1 medium onion, chopped (about 1 cup)
2 carrots, chopped (about ¾ cup)
¼ cup sherry
4 to 5 cloves garlic, minced

6 sprigs fresh thyme tied into a bundle
   (or ½ teaspoon dried)
1 bay leaf
3 cups beef broth
2 cups red wine such as Shiraz,
   Zinfandel or Pinot Noir
14½ ounces diced tomatoes, undrained
1 tablespoon Balsamic vinegar

Preheat the oven to 350°F. Heat ¼ cup of the olive oil in a large Dutch oven over medium. Pat the short ribs dry with a paper towel and season with salt and pepper. Place the short ribs in the pot and brown. Remove the ribs from the pot and set aside. Add the onions and carrots to the pot and deglaze with the sherry, making sure to scrape the browned bits from the bottom of the pot. Cook the vegetables until the sherry is absorbed, about 4 to 5 minutes. Add the remaining tablespoon of olive oil to the pot and stir in the garlic, thyme and bay leaf. Add the broth, wine, tomatoes with juice and vinegar. Add the short ribs back in with any reserved juices; bring to a boil. Cover, place in the oven and cook for 2 to 2½ hours. Remove from the oven and place on the stove top. Remove the short ribs and most of the vegetables from the broth; cover and keep warm. Discard the thyme and bay leaf. Heat the broth mixture over medium-high and stir occasionally until thickened and reduced by half, about 30 minutes. Serve the warm short ribs with sauce.

194

BEEF TENDERLOIN *with* GORGONZOLA SAUCE

SERVES 10 *to* 12

Beef tenderloin is perhaps the dinner party entrée that most says "special."
Here, creamy gorgonzola is a good match for the rich beef tenderloin. When you choose beef tenderloin
or filet mignon steaks, look for bright red meat with evenly distributed marbling.

1 beef tenderloin (about 4 to 5 pounds), trimmed
1 tablespoon unsalted butter, softened
coarse salt and freshly ground pepper

Gorgonzola Sauce:
4 cups heavy whipping cream
2 ounces crumbled Gorgonzola cheese (about ½ cup)

3 tablespoons freshly grated Parmesan cheese
¾ teaspoon coarse salt, plus additional
½ teaspoon freshly ground pepper, plus additional
3 tablespoons minced fresh parsley

Set the tenderloin out for 1 hour to come to room temperature. Carefully bring the cream to a full boil in a heavy saucepan over medium-high heat. Lower heat and simmer, stirring frequently, for 55 to 60 minutes or until the cream has thickened. Remove the pan from heat and add the cheeses, salt, pepper and parsley, stirring rapidly until the cheeses are melted; set aside. Preheat the oven to 500°F. Place the tenderloin in a roasting pan and pat dry with a paper towel. Coat the top and sides of the tenderloin with the butter; season with salt and pepper. Roast for 20 minutes, then turn off the oven and leave the tenderloin in for 30 more minutes (do not open the oven door). Slice the tenderloin and serve with the warm *Gorgonzola Sauce*.

SPINACH *and* PROSCIUTTO STUFFED FLANK STEAK

SERVES 6 *to* 8

This is a loaded flank steak to serve at room temperature on the patio.
Butchers can simplify preparation by pounding the steak for you.

1 flank steak (about 1¾ to 2 pounds),
   trimmed and pounded to ½-inch thickness
coarse salt and freshly ground pepper
¼ cup extra virgin olive oil, divided, plus additional
5 ounces fresh spinach (about 8 cups)
½ cup fresh bread crumbs

½ cup freshly grated Parmesan cheese
2 to 3 cloves garlic, minced
3 ounces prosciutto, thinly sliced
3 large ripe tomatoes, thickly sliced
6 (8-inch) lengths kitchen twine

Preheat the oven to 350°F. Season the steak with salt and pepper; set aside. Heat 1 tablespoon of the olive oil in a pan over medium; add the spinach and cook until just wilted. Transfer the spinach to ice water to cool. Drain and squeeze out all of the excess water; set aside. In a large bowl, mix together the bread crumbs, cheese and garlic. Add the spinach to the bread crumb mixture and mix well.

To assemble the flank steak, layer the prosciutto over the entire steak and then spread the spinach mixture evenly over the prosciutto. Starting at one end of the meat, roll the long side inward; tie the roll with cooking twine at 2-inch intervals and trim the twine. Brush the meat generously with the remaining olive oil and place in a baking pan. Bake the meat for 50 minutes for medium-rare or 60 minutes for well-done. Remove from the oven and allow to rest for 10 minutes before removing the twine. To serve, slice the meat and arrange the slices down the center of a platter. Arrange the tomato slices around the steak; drizzle olive oil over the tomatoes and season with salt and pepper.

FILET MIGNON *with* CHANTERELLES

SERVES 4

If food can be romantic, this is the dish.

4 filet mignon steaks (about 6 ounces each),
   about 1½ inches thick
coarse salt and freshly ground pepper
4 tablespoons (½ stick) butter
4 cups sliced chanterelle or portobello mushrooms
2 cups dry white wine

2 cups heavy whipping cream
2 teaspoons chopped fresh thyme, plus additional
½ teaspoon coarse salt
whole peppercorns (optional)

Season the steaks with salt and pepper. Preheat the grill or a grill pan. Grill the steaks to medium rare; set aside to rest. Melt the butter in a large skillet over medium heat. Add the mushrooms and sauté for 5 minutes. Add the wine and reduce the liquid by half. Add the cream, thyme and salt; simmer until the sauce has thickened. Add the steaks to the skillet to warm if necessary. Serve the steaks with the sauce spooned over the top and garnished with thyme and whole peppercorns, if desired.

195

Balsamic Glazed Steaks, PAGE 197

PORK ROAST *with* AUTUMN FRUIT

SERVES 6 *to* 8

Fruit-topped loin of pork makes a delicious entrée for an autumn dinner.
Serve piping hot in its own juices; served cold, the tartness of the fruit is slightly accentuated.

3 pound pork loin roast, butterflied
½ cup chopped dried apricots
½ cup chopped dried figs
⅓ cup dried cranberries
½ cup peeled and chopped apples
½ cup apple juice
1½ cups chicken broth, divided

6 fresh sage leaves, chopped
1½ teaspoons peeled and finely grated fresh ginger
1 clove garlic, minced
coarse salt and freshly ground pepper
vegetable oil
1 teaspoon cornstarch
6 (10-inch) lengths of kitchen twine

Remove the roast from the refrigerator about 1 hour before roasting. Preheat the oven to 375°F. Combine the dried fruits, apples, apple juice and 1 cup of the broth in a small saucepan. Add the sage, ginger and garlic. Season with salt and pepper. Cook over medium-low heat until the dried fruits are reconstituted and the apples are tender, about 30 minutes (the liquid will have reduced). Place the pork loin in a roasting pan and spoon three-fourths of the fruit mixture on top of the meat along one of the long sides, leaving a 1-inch edge on the ends. Fold the loin into a cylinder and tie with kitchen twine at 2-inch intervals to secure; trim the excess twine and discard. Rub the roast with oil and season generously with salt and pepper. Spoon the remaining fruit over the pork loin. Roast for about 45 minutes or until desired doneness. Transfer the pork loin to a cutting board, reserving the juices. Let the pork stand for 10 minutes before slicing.

While the pork loin is resting, make the sauce. Mix together 1½ teaspoons of water and the cornstarch in a small bowl; set aside. In a saucepan over medium-high heat, combine the reserved juices, the remaining ½ cup of broth and the cornstarch mixture, stirring frequently, until desired consistency. Slice the pork loin and place on a serving dish or individual plates. Drizzle with the sauce and spoon the cooked fruit over the pork.

a1

SLOW COOKED HERB CRUSTED PORK ROAST

SERVES 6

This delicious roast—crispy on the outside and tender on the inside—is its own reward for planning ahead.

2 tablespoons finely chopped fresh sage
2 tablespoons fresh rosemary
10 cloves garlic, peeled
1 tablespoon fennel seeds
1½ tablespoons coarse salt

1 tablespoon freshly ground pepper
1 tablespoon dry white wine
1 tablespoon olive oil
6 pound pork shoulder Boston roast, untied
kitchen twine

Preheat the oven to 275°F. Blend together the sage, rosemary, garlic, fennel seeds, salt and pepper in a food processor until a thick paste forms. With the processor running, add the wine and olive oil, and blend until well combined. If necessary, trim the fat from the top of the roast, leaving a ⅛-inch thick layer of fat. Using a small sharp knife, make 3 small incisions, each about 1-inch long and 1-inch deep, on each side of the roast; fill each with about 1 teaspoon of the herb paste. Spread the remaining herb paste over the roast, concentrating on the boned side. Tie the roast with kitchen twine at 2-inch intervals. Place the pork, fat side up, in a deep roasting pan and roast on the middle rack of the oven for 6 hours. Transfer to a cutting board and let stand for 15 minutes. Discard the string and cut the roast into thick slices to serve.

menu sampler

MARKET SUPPER

*Warm Goat Cheese
with Tomato Coulis*

Honey Roasted Root Vegetables

Creamy Pumpkin Polenta

*Winter Salad with
Poppy Seed Dressing*

Marvelous Mushrooms

Pear Brioche Bread Pudding

∾

FARM-FRESH FEAST

*Avocado Cucumber Soup
with Cilantro*

*Camembert and Pecan Quesadillas
with Pineapple Salsa*

Texas Corn Pudding

Sliced Farm Fresh Tomatoes

Cool Meyer Lemon Pudding

Gingered Sugar Snap Peas, PAGE 208
Sesame Citrus Sea Bass, PAGE 161

GINGERED SUGAR SNAP PEAS
SERVES 4
The zing of ginger complements the sweetness of peas in this dish, which can be ready in a matter of minutes.

1 tablespoon olive oil
1 pound sugar snap peas, strings removed

1 tablespoon peeled and finely chopped fresh ginger
coarse salt and freshly ground pepper

Heat the olive oil in a 12-inch skillet over medium. Add the peas and ginger, and cook for 4 to 5 minutes until the peas begin to brown, stirring occasionally. Add ¼ cup of water and cook about 2 more minutes while stirring and scraping the ginger from the bottom of the skillet. The peas should be crisp-tender. Transfer to a serving plate with a slotted spoon and season with salt and pepper.

LEMONY GREEN BEANS *and* MUSHROOMS
SERVES 4
*These tart, lemony beans are cooked with cremini mushrooms, which are more flavorful than more common
button or white mushrooms though similar in size and appearance. Interestingly, portobello mushrooms are actually giant creminis.*

1½ pounds green beans, washed and trimmed
2 tablespoons butter
8 ounces cremini mushrooms, cleaned and sliced

coarse salt and freshly ground pepper
zest and juice of 1 lemon

Blanch the beans in boiling water and cook for about 4 to 6 minutes until tender but still bright green (do not overcook). Cool the beans under cold running water, drain and set aside. Heat the butter in a medium sauté pan over medium-low. Add the mushrooms and cook for 2 to 3 minutes over medium heat. Do not stir. Season generously with salt and pepper. Mix well and continue cooking for 2 minutes. Add the beans, lemon zest and juice; cover and cook 3 minutes. Serve immediately.

SAUTÉED BROCCOLI RABE
SERVES 4 *to* 5
*Also known as rapini, broccoli rabe (actually a member of the turnip family) is a leafy green stalk
with scattered clusters of small broccoli-like florets. In fact, blanched broccoli florets can be substituted for the broccoli rabe in this dish.*

1 pound broccoli rabe, tough stems peeled
1 tablespoon extra virgin olive oil
2 cloves garlic, coarsely chopped

1 shallot, thinly sliced
coarse salt
¼ teaspoon crushed red pepper

Blanch the broccoli rabe in a large pot of boiling salted water until crisp-tender, about 2 minutes. Drain and transfer to a bowl of ice water to cool. Drain again and pat dry. Heat the olive oil in a heavy large skillet over medium. Add the garlic and shallots, and sauté until fragrant, about 1 minute. Add the broccoli rabe and sauté until heated through, about 4 minutes. Remove from heat. Season with salt and the crushed red pepper. Transfer to a warm platter and serve.

BALSAMIC GLAZED CARROTS

SERVES 4 *to* 6

The natural sweetness of the carrots is intensified by the sweet, tart glaze.
Serve this earthy side dish with your favorite roasted meats.

2 tablespoons olive oil
2 tablespoons unsalted butter
1 pound fresh baby carrots, peeled
2 large shallots, thinly sliced
1 red bell pepper, seeded and diced (about 1 cup)

3 tablespoons Balsamic vinegar
1½ tablespoons light brown sugar
½ teaspoon coarse salt
¼ teaspoon freshly ground pepper
2 tablespoons finely chopped fresh parsley

Heat the olive oil and butter in a large skillet over medium-high. Sauté the carrots, shallots and bell pepper until the carrots are tender and slightly browned, stirring occasionally. Stir in the vinegar, brown sugar, salt and pepper. Reduce heat and cook for 5 minutes or until the liquid is reduced and the vegetables begin to glaze. Remove from heat, garnish with the parsley and serve immediately.

HONEY ROASTED ROOT VEGETABLES

SERVES 4 *to* 6

These humble vegetables turn sweet and tender when roasted with vinegar, honey and seasonings—
they are perfect for pairing with grilled meat and poultry.

2 pounds of a variety of root vegetables, peeled and cut
    into 1-inch pieces (carrots, celery root, parsnips,
    rutabaga, turnips)
1 pound butternut squash, peeled, seeded and cut
    into 1-inch pieces
4 fingerling potatoes, unpeeled and cut into 1-inch pieces
3 shallots, peeled and quartered

1 head of garlic, cloves separated, peeled and thickly sliced
3 tablespoons extra virgin olive oil
2 tablespoons sherry vinegar
1 tablespoon orange blossom honey
coarse salt and freshly ground pepper
2 tablespoons finely chopped fresh Italian flat leaf parsley

213

Preheat the oven to 400°F. Toss the vegetables with the olive oil, vinegar and honey in a large bowl until thoroughly coated. Season generously with salt and pepper. Spread the vegetable mixture in one layer on a large rimmed baking sheet. Bake until tender and brown, about 45 minutes to 1 hour, stirring occasionally. Sprinkle with the parsley and toss before transferring to a serving dish.

> ❧ ORANGE BLOSSOM HONEY ❧
>
> *Made by bees that get nectar from orange blossoms, this honey is sweet, fragrant and delicately citrusy. It adds a special nuance to fruit, oatmeal, yogurt, ice cream, waffles and toast, and even meat glazes.*

ROASTED BEETS *with* ORANGE

SERVES 4

Use both red and golden beets for a dramatic side dish that pops with color and flavor.

1 pound fresh red beets (about 6 beets)
zest of 1 orange, divided
1 teaspoon coarse salt
½ teaspoon freshly ground pepper

2 tablespoons olive oil
2 tablespoons freshly squeezed orange juice
3 tablespoons chopped fresh cilantro,
    Italian flat leaf parsley or mint

Preheat the oven to 450°F. Trim the stem ends of the beets, leaving about 1 inch intact; leave root ends untouched. Place the beets on a sheet of foil and sprinkle with half of the orange zest and all of the salt and pepper. Close the foil tightly and bake until the beets are tender when pierced with the tip of a knife, approximately 1½ hours. Remove the beets from the oven and allow to cool enough to handle easily. Trim the ends of the beets and slip off the skins. Quarter each beet and cut into ½-inch slices. Whisk together the olive oil, the remaining half of the orange zest, the orange juice and fresh herbs in a serving bowl. Add the beets and toss. Season with additional salt and pepper, if desired. Serve warm.

CILANTRO RICE

COURTESY *of* CHEF MICHAEL CORDÚA, CORDÚA RESTAURANT GROUP

SERVES 10 *to* 12

This versatile side dish is good company for anything from enchiladas to grilled meats and seafood. Delicious with "The Churrasco"
Beef Tenderloin (page 193). Prepared chicken base is a concentrated paste or powder, usually found on the soup aisle near bouillon and broth.

2 tablespoons chicken base
1 teaspoon minced garlic
6 ounces fresh cilantro (about 1 bunch)
1 quart chicken stock
2 tablespoons corn oil

1 large onion, diced to ¼ inch
2½ cups rice
5 pounds tomatoes, diced to ¼ inch
2 tablespoons salt

Purée the chicken base, garlic, cilantro and stock. Place over high heat in a large saucepan and bring to a boil. Heat the corn oil in a braising pan; add the onion and cook until lightly browned. Add the rice and stir over heat until the rice is completely covered with oil. Pour in the boiling ingredients, cover and steep for 18 to 20 minutes; add the tomatoes and salt after 7 minutes. Continue cooking until the liquid is absorbed and the rice is fluffy.

....

BULGUR WHEAT PILAF *with* CURRANTS

SERVES 6

With a hint of sweetness and a nutty texture, this dish pairs well with grilled or roasted meat like lamb or pork.
To make it ahead, cool the pilaf, cover and refrigerate. Before serving, bring to room temperature, fluff with a fork and garnish.

1 tablespoon olive oil
½ cup chopped celery
¼ cup chopped onion
1 clove garlic, minced
¼ to ½ cup dried currants
1 cup apple juice
1 cup chicken broth

1 teaspoon cumin seed
1 teaspoon curry powder
½ teaspoon coarse salt
¼ teaspoon ground allspice
1 cup uncooked bulgur wheat
2 tablespoons minced fresh parsley
¼ cup thinly sliced green onions

Heat the olive oil in a sauté pan over medium-high. Cook the celery and onion for 5 minutes or until tender. Add the garlic and sauté for 1 more minute. Stir in the currants, apple juice, broth, cumin seed, curry, salt and allspice. Bring to a boil and stir in the bulgur wheat. Cover, reduce heat to low and simmer for 15 to 20 minutes or until the liquid is absorbed, stirring occasionally. Remove from heat. Fluff the pilaf with a fork and cool for 5 to 10 minutes. Fluff again and top with the parsley and green onions.

....

SAVORY ROSEMARY CRANBERRY COMPOTE

SERVES 10 *to* 12

This flavorful twist on a holiday classic is an obvious choice for turkey. It is equally good with beef and lamb;
as an appetizer served with crackers and cheese; or as a way to make grilled cheese something special.
Freeze some fresh cranberries so you can make this compote year round.

2 cups dry, spicy red wine such as Zinfandel,
   Syrah or Pinot Noir
½ cup dried cherries
12 ounces frozen dark sweet cherries

12 ounces fresh cranberries, picked through
1 cup lightly packed light brown sugar
2 tablespoons minced fresh rosemary
1 tablespoon allspice

This recipe requires advance preparation. Combine the wine and dried cherries in a deep saucepan. Boil until reduced to approximately ⅔ cup, about 10 to 12 minutes. In the meantime, halve each of the frozen cherries. Add the frozen cherries and the remaining ingredients to the saucepan. Bring to a boil, reduce heat to medium and cover until the cranberries burst, about 7 to 8 minutes. Refrigerate for at least 3 hours to allow the flavors to develop. Serve at any temperature.

SMOKED GOUDA MASHED SWEET POTATOES
SERVES 6
This easy new way to enjoy sweet potatoes can be a colorful alternative to regular mashed potatoes.
Increase the cayenne pepper for a spicier flavor.

4 tablespoons butter
3 tablespoons heavy whipping cream, divided
½ teaspoon coarse salt
1 teaspoon sugar
⅛ teaspoon cayenne pepper

2 pounds sweet potatoes, peeled and cut into ¼-inch slices
½ cup (2 ounces) shredded smoked Gouda cheese
6 strips bacon, cooked crisp and crumbled
2 green onions, chopped

Heat the butter, 2 tablespoons of the cream, the salt, sugar, cayenne and sweet potatoes in a large sauté pan over medium-low. Once the butter has melted, stir to coat the potatoes. Reduce the heat to low, cover and cook until the potatoes are very tender, about 30 to 40 minutes, stirring occasionally. Remove from heat and add the cheese and the remaining tablespoon of cream; cover for 1 to 2 minutes until the cheese melts. Mix thoroughly to mash the potatoes. Top with the bacon and onions just before serving.

POMMES FRITES *with* TRUFFLE OIL *and* PARMESAN
SERVES 6
Infused with flavor, these twice-fried pommes frites are an extraordinary take on traditional fries.
For pommes frites that are crispy on the outside and tender on the inside, follow the temperature directions exactly.
For a different taste, replace the coarse salt and truffle oil with a flavored salt.

6 large white Russet potatoes
2 quarts peanut oil
coarse salt

2 to 3 teaspoons truffle oil
freshly shaved Parmesan cheese

215

This recipe requires advance preparation. Cut the potatoes lengthwise into ¼-inch strips. Cover with water in a bowl and refrigerate overnight or at least 12 hours to remove the starch. Drain the potatoes well before frying. Heat the peanut oil to 370°F in a Dutch oven or deep fryer. Add one-third of the potatoes and cook for 3 minutes. Carefully remove and set aside on a paper towel-lined plate. When the oil reaches 370°F again, cook a second batch of frites and repeat again. For the second fry, reheat the oil to 380°F, add half of the frites, and cook for 4 minutes or until golden. Remove from the oil, drain on brown paper bags and immediately sprinkle with salt. Repeat with the other half. Drizzle with the truffle oil, sprinkle with cheese and serve immediately.

> ∽ FLAVORED SALTS ∾
>
> *Buy flavored salts or have fun making them at home.*
> *Add chopped fresh rosemary or thyme to coarse salt.*
> *Lavender flowers, Greek oregano and crushed red pepper*
> *are other interesting alternatives. A rule of thumb:*
> *add 1 tablespoon of herbs or 1 teaspoon of spices for*
> *every 4 tablespoons of coarse salt.*

Creamy Pumpkin Polenta, PAGE 219

CREAMY PUMPKIN POLENTA

SERVES 8

Cinnamon, basil and pumpkin combine beautifully in this melt in your mouth polenta.

2½ cups milk
2 cups water or vegetable broth
¾ cup canned pure pumpkin
2 teaspoons coarse salt
1¼ cups instant dry polenta

1 cup freshly grated Parmigiano-Reggiano cheese
¼ cup mascarpone cheese
¼ teaspoon cinnamon
2 tablespoons chopped fresh basil
¼ cup freshly shaved Parmigiano-Reggiano cheese

Bring the milk and water to a boil in a large saucepan over medium heat. Whisk in the pumpkin and salt. Reduce heat to low and gradually whisk in the polenta. Cook for 1 minute or until thickened and remove from heat. Add the grated Parmigiano-Reggiano, mascarpone, cinnamon and basil, stirring until the cheese melts. The consistency should be thick but creamy. Top with the shaved Parmigiano-Reggiano and serve.

CARROT PUDDING

SERVES 8

Creamy, light and sweet, this simple pudding complements a hearty beef roast or simple roasted chicken.

2 pounds carrots, peeled and cut into 1-inch pieces
¾ cup (1½ sticks) butter, melted
6 eggs
1 cup sugar

6 tablespoons all-purpose flour
2 teaspoons baking powder
2 teaspoons pure vanilla extract

Preheat the oven to 350°F. Place the carrots in a medium saucepan and cover with water. Bring to a boil over high heat and simmer for about 10 minutes until fork tender. Drain the carrots and let cool slightly. Purée the carrots in a food processor. Add the butter and the remaining ingredients, and mix until well blended. Pour the mixture into a 9 by 13-inch baking dish and bake for 45 minutes.

REFRIED WHITE BEANS

SERVES 6

This dish, a reinterpretation of a time-honored staple, does not have to be part of a Mexican menu to be special.
A drizzle of truffle oil or a dash of rosemary salt makes an excellent garnish.

1 tablespoon olive or safflower oil
1 small white onion, finely chopped
coarse salt and freshly ground pepper
3 large cloves roasted garlic

30 ounces canned white beans
  (navy beans work well), drained
½ to ⅔ cup dry white wine (or chicken broth)
chopped fresh parsley

☙ ROASTING GARLIC ❧

Roasted garlic is available at most grocery stores. To make your own, cut the top off a whole head of garlic, drizzle with olive oil and wrap tightly with foil. Bake at 350°F for 20 minutes or until soft. Roasted garlic adds flavor to a variety of dishes and also makes a distinctive spread.

Heat the oil in a medium saucepan over medium-high. Add the onions and a pinch of salt, and sauté until transparent. Add the garlic and sauté for an additional 45 seconds. Add the beans and remove from heat. Mash the beans until fairly smooth using an immersion blender (or purée in a food processor and return to saucepan). Add the wine and stir to combine. Bring to a boil, lower heat and allow the mixture to reduce and thicken. Stir occasionally for about 15 minutes. Once the mixture has reduced, season with salt and pepper. Remove from heat and the beans will continue to thicken slightly. Garnish with parsley before serving.

menu sampler

SUGARPLUM COOKIE SWAP

White Hot Chocolate
Shortbread Cookies with Perfect Icing
Soft Ginger Cookies
Chocolate Crinkle Cookies

&

THE CHOCOLATE BAR

Chocolate Martini
Chocolate Grand Marnier Truffle
Soufflés with Caramel Sauce
Brandied Chocolate
Cherry Bread Pudding
Hazelnut Dream Cookies
Chocolate Fondue Sauce with Fruit

Over-the-Top Fudgy Brownies, PAGE 225

Blackberry Shortbread Bars, PAGE 225

OVER-THE-TOP FUDGY BROWNIES

MAKES 32 BROWNIES

These espresso-laced brownies are designed to please a grownup palate.
Because you will make them with your favorite candy bar (Milky Way®, Snickers®, York Peppermint Patties®), these could
easily become your signature treat. Make them even fudgier with the Chocolate Fondue Sauce (recipe below).

2 cups (4 sticks) unsalted butter
28 ounces semi-sweet chocolate chips, divided
6 ounces unsweetened chocolate
6 eggs
3 tablespoons instant espresso
2 tablespoons pure vanilla extract

2¼ cups sugar
1¼ cups all-purpose flour, divided
1 tablespoon baking powder
1 teaspoon salt
2 cups chopped walnuts (optional)
11 to 12 ounces Milky Way®, coarsely chopped

This recipe requires overnight refrigeration after baking. Preheat the oven to 350°F. Line a 9 by 13-inch metal (not glass) pan with foil, leaving enough foil to hang over the edges of the pan. Butter and flour the foil; set aside. In a double boiler (or a large bowl set over a pot of simmering water), melt the butter, 16 ounces of the chocolate chips and the unsweetened chocolate. Stir to combine, then allow to cool slightly. In a large bowl, whisk together the eggs, espresso, vanilla and sugar. Starting in small amounts, add the warm chocolate mixture to the egg mixture; allow to cool to room temperature. In another bowl, sift together 1 cup of the flour, the baking powder and salt; stir into the cooled chocolate-egg mixture until just combined. In another medium bowl, toss the walnuts and the remaining 12 ounces of chocolate chips with the remaining ¼ cup of flour; add to the chocolate-egg-flour mixture.

Pour half of the batter into the prepared pan and smooth the top. Arrange the candy in a single layer over the batter, making sure the candy reaches the edges of the pan. Top with the remaining batter and smooth. Bake for 35 minutes; although the brownies will not be firm, do not overbake. Allow to cool, then refrigerate overnight. Remove the brownies from the pan using the foil overhang and cut into small squares with a serrated bread knife. Store in the refrigerator.

∽ CHOCOLATE FONDUE SAUCE ∾

1¼ cups heavy whipping cream or light cream
1 teaspoon pure vanilla extract
2 tablespoons butter
6 ounces 70% cacao bittersweet chocolate bars, chopped
6 ounces milk chocolate bars, chopped
2 to 4 tablespoons Kahlúa® or Tia Maria® (optional)

In a medium saucepan over medium heat, combine the cream, vanilla and butter, and heat until the mixture just simmers. Remove the mixture from heat and stir in the chocolate and liqueur until smooth. Serve with bite-size pieces of angel food cake, kiwi, strawberries, pineapple chunks or orange sections.

BLACKBERRY SHORTBREAD BARS

MAKES 24 BARS

Make these anytime you want the flavor of two old-fashioned favorites—a fruit cobbler and a bar cookie.
These sturdy treats are great for gift giving or tucking into a lunchbox.

Crust:
3 cups all-purpose flour
1¼ cups sugar
¼ teaspoon salt
1½ cups (3 sticks) unsalted butter, chilled

Filling:
2 eggs, whisked
½ cup sugar
½ cup sour cream
⅓ cup all-purpose flour
16 ounces frozen blackberries, thawed

Crust: Preheat the oven to 350°F. Prepare a 9 by 13-inch baking pan with butter or cooking spray; set aside. Combine the flour, sugar and salt in a food processor for about 45 seconds. Cut the butter into ½-inch cubes and process with the flour mixture for 30 seconds or until the butter is evenly distributed but the mixture is still crumbly. Reserve 1½ cups of the crust mixture to use as a topping. Press the remaining crust mixture firmly into the bottom of the prepared pan. Bake for about 25 minutes or until golden brown; allow to cool for at least 10 minutes before adding the filling.

Filling: Combine the eggs, sugar, sour cream and flour in a large bowl. Fold in the blackberries. Spoon the fruit filling evenly over the crust and sprinkle the reserved crust mixture over the filling. Bake for 45 to 55 minutes or until the top is lightly browned. Let cool for at least 1 hour before cutting into bars.

CHOCOLATE CHIP BISCOTTI

MAKES 40 BISCOTTI

This is a softer version of biscotti. Make them fun for special occasions (for birthday biscotti, sprinkle with multicolored nonpareils instead of sugar) or introduce different flavors (almond extract in place of vanilla; chopped slivered almonds instead of sprinkling sugar).

1 cup (2 sticks) unsalted butter, softened
½ cup sugar, plus additional
1¼ cups light brown sugar
2 teaspoons pure vanilla extract
6 eggs

5½ cups all-purpose flour
2 tablespoons baking powder
½ teaspoon salt
2 cups semi-sweet chocolate chips

Preheat the oven to 350°F. Line a cookie sheet with parchment paper. Cream the butter, sugar and brown sugar with a mixer on medium speed. Add in the vanilla and eggs, and mix well. On slow speed, gradually add in the flour, baking powder and salt until just blended. Add the chocolate chips to the mixture and stir with a spoon. Knead the dough on a lightly floured surface and form into a ball. Divide the dough into four equal parts and roll each into a 12-inch long loaf. Place the loaves on the prepared cookie sheet approximately 3 inches apart. Lightly brush the top of each loaf with water and sprinkle lightly with sugar. Bake for 25 to 30 minutes or until golden brown. Remove from the oven. Very carefully transfer or slide each loaf off the cookie sheet and onto a cutting board (use the parchment paper or long spatulas to support the loaves to ensure they do not break or crumble). Let the loaves cool for about 20 minutes. Cut each cooled loaf diagonally into ½-inch wide slices. Place the sliced cookies on their sides in a single layer on the same parchment-lined cookie sheet. Bake again for 12 to 15 minutes or until lightly browned. Remove from the oven and cool on a wire rack.

CHOCOLATE SNAPS

MAKES 6 DOZEN COOKIES

These crispy chocolate cookies are a fun treat to make with kids. They also make sweet gifts.

1 cup (2 sticks) unsalted butter
1½ cups sugar, divided
1 egg
2 cups semi-sweet chocolate chips, melted
½ cup corn syrup

1½ teaspoons pure vanilla extract
4 cups all-purpose flour
4 teaspoons baking soda
2 teaspoons cinnamon
½ teaspoon salt

Preheat the oven to 350°F. Mix together the butter, 1 cup of the sugar and the egg in a large bowl. Beat with a mixer on low speed until creamy. Blend in the melted chocolate, corn syrup and vanilla. In a separate bowl, combine the flour, baking soda, cinnamon and salt. Add the dry mixture to the chocolate mixture and mix well. Place the remaining ½ cup of sugar in a small bowl. Shape the dough into 1-inch balls and roll in the sugar. Bake for 12 minutes on an ungreased cookie sheet.